j020 D611
**Discovering careers for
your future.**

DISCOVERING CAREERS FOR YOUR FUTURE

library and information science

Ferguson

An imprint of Infobase Publishing

Discovering Careers for Your Future: Library and Information Science

Ferguson
An imprint of Infobase Publishing
132 West 31st Street
New York NY 10001

Library of Congress Cataloging-in-Publication Data

Discovering careers for your future. Library and information science.
        p. cm.
    Includes bibliographical references and index.
    ISBN-13: 987-0-8160-7282-8 (acid-free paper)
    ISBN-10: 0-8160-7282-5 (acid-free paper) 1. Library science—Vocational guidance—Juvenile literature. 2. Information science—Vocational guidance—Juuvenile literature. I. Ferguson Publishing. II. Title: Library and information science.
    Z682.35.V62D57 2008
    020'.23—dc22
                                        2007040863

Ferguson books are available at special discounts when purchased in bulk quantities for businesses, associations, institutions, or sales promotions. Please call our Special Sales Department in New York at (212) 967-8800 or (800) 322-8755.

You can find Ferguson on the World Wide Web at http://www.fergpubco.com

Text design by Mary Susan Ryan-Flynn
Cover design by Jooyoung An

Printed in the United States of America

EB MSRF 10 9 8 7 6 5 4 3 2 1

This book is printed on acid-free paper.

Contents

Introduction

You may not have decided yet what you want to be in the future. And you don't have to decide right away. You do know that right now you are interested in library and information science. Do any of the statements below describe you? If so, you may want to begin thinking about what a career in library and information science might mean for you.

___I love to read.
___I spend a lot of time in my school or community library.
___I am good at organizing things.
___I like to make lists of books, music, and movies to suggest to others.
___I love helping people find information.
___I enjoy working with computers.
___I like keeping track of information.
___I enjoy doing research.
___I like to teach people.
___I like to repair old books and magazines.
___I enjoy learning about new technology.

Discovering Careers for Your Future: Library and Information Science is a book about careers in library science, from archivists and information brokers to librarians and research assistants.

This book describes many possibilities for future careers in library and information science. Read through it to see the variety of careers that are available. For example, if you are interested in working as a librarian, you should read about the many career specialties that are available such as acquisitions librarians, children's librarians, corporate librarians, film and video librarians, law librarians, medical librarians, and music librarians. If you are interested in restoring old or damaged books, you will want to read the chapter on book conservators. If you like doing research, you will want to read the chapters on information brokers and research assistants. If you are interested in working with library and information technology, you will want to read the chapters on database specialists and library media specialists. Perhaps you want to teach library science. If so, then you should read the chapter on college professors, library science. Go ahead and explore!

What Do Library and Information Science Workers Do?

The first section of each chapter begins with a heading such as "What Library Media Specialists Do" or "What Archivists Do." This section tells what it's like to work at a particular job. It also describes typical responsibilities and working conditions. Which library and information science professionals work at community libraries? Which ones work at home? Which ones work on college campuses or at corporations? This section answers these and other questions.

How Do I Become a Library and Information Science Worker?

The section called "Education and Training" tells you what schooling you need for employment in each job—a high school diploma, training at a junior college, a college degree, or more. It also talks about what high school and college courses you should take to prepare for the field.

How Much Do Library and Information Science Workers Earn?

The Earnings section gives the average salary figures for the job described in the chapter. These figures give you a general idea of how much money people with this job can make. Keep in mind that many people really earn more or less than the amounts cited here because actual salaries depend on many factors, such as the size of the company, the location of the company, and the amount of education, training, and experience you have. Generally, but not always, larger companies located in major cities pay more than smaller ones in smaller cities and towns, and people with more education, training, and experience earn more. Also remember that these figures are current or recent averages. They will probably be different by the time you are ready to enter the workforce.

What Will the Future Be Like for Library and Information Science Workers?

The Outlook section discusses the employment outlook for the career: whether the total number of people employed in this career will increase or decrease in the coming years and whether jobs in this field will be easy or hard to find. These predictions are based on economic conditions, the size and makeup of the population, foreign competition, and new technology. Terms such as "about as fast as the average" and "slower than the average" are terms used by the U.S. Department of Labor to describe job growth predicted by government data.

Keep in mind that these predictions are general statements. No one knows for sure what the future will be like. Also remember that the employment outlook is a general statement about an industry and does not necessarily apply to everyone. A determined and talented person may be able to find a job in an industry or career with the worst outlook. And a person without ambition and the proper training will find it difficult to find a job in even a booming industry or career field.

Where Can I Find More Information?

Each chapter includes a sidebar called "For More Info." It lists resources that you can contact to find out more about the field and careers in the field. You will find names, addresses, phone numbers, e-mail addresses, and Web sites of library science–oriented associations and organizations.

Extras

Every chapter has a few extras. There are photos that show library and information science workers in action. There are sidebars and notes on ways to explore the field, fun facts, or lists of Web sites and books that might be helpful. At the end of the book you will find a Glossary, an Index, and a Browse and Learn More section. The Glossary gives brief definitions of words that you may not know relating to education, career training, or employment. The Index includes all the job titles mentioned in the book. The Browse and Learn More section lists general library and information science books and Web sites to explore.

It's not too soon to think about your future. We hope you discover several possible career choices in library and information science. Happy hunting!

Acquisitions Librarians

What Acquisitions Librarians Do

Acquisitions librarians build and maintain library collections. These include print references such as books and periodicals; digital references such as CD-ROMs, DVDs, and e-publications; and music, art, and other resources. Acquisitions librarians work for all types of libraries, though most work in academic libraries. They are also called *collection development librarians* and *collection development specialists*.

Acquisitions librarians work with library directors to assess the needs of the library and determine how to best spend funds that are available to buy library materials. They rely on reviews in trade publications, information gathered at trade shows, suggestions from patrons, and the Internet to help them make decisions on what to buy.

Changing technology has created new challenges for acquisitions librarians. Not only has information become more readily accessible because of the Internet, it also comes in new formats. Acquisitions librarians must determine what format is best for each resource. For example, they may choose to purchase a magazine subscription in online format to save storage space or to allow more people to use the resource. Or they may prefer hard copies of a popular reference material if there is a shortage of computer terminals in the library.

In order to know what to purchase, acquisitions librarians must first be

Did You Know?

The Association for Library Collections and Technical Services, the major professional association for acquisitions librarians, has nearly 5,000 members. According to the association, 75 percent of its members work in academic libraries and 11 percent in public libraries. The remaining 14 percent work in special libraries and other settings.

EXPLORING

○ Read books and magazines about librarianship.

○ Visit the Web sites of library associations, such as the American Library Association (see For More Info).

○ Visit the Web sites of library acquisitions departments to learn about issues that affect acquisitions librarians.

○ Ask your school librarian about the acquisitions or collection development aspects of his or her job.

○ A librarian, teacher, or guidance counselor may be able to arrange an information interview with an acquisitions librarian.

familiar with the resources that are currently in the library. They meet with cataloging and circulation librarians to find out which items are most popular and which ones might need to be replaced due to wear and tear or for other reasons. Acquisitions librarians may even help cataloging librarians catalog and maintain existing resources, conduct repair work on used items, and assess which books, magazines, and other items need to be replaced.

When they do not have enough funds to make new purchases, some acquisitions librarians try to find other sources of funding. They may write grants to obtain public or private funding or lead donation drives to add to their collection.

Education and Training

In high school, take college-preparatory classes in business, science, English, mathematics, and foreign languages. You should also take as many computer classes as you can. Because technology has greatly changed the way we receive and store information, those familiar with computers and related technology will have the greatest professional success.

You will need a master's degree in library science (MLS), a master's degree in library information service, or a master's degree in information science to work as an acquisitions librarian. Some acquisitions librarians may even hold a Ph.D. in information or library science. A graduate degree from a program accredited by the American Library Association is highly regarded by employers.

The Smallest Book in the World

Talk about tiny! Anton Chekhov's *Chameleon,* the smallest book in the world (at least according to the *Guinness Book of World Records*) measures just .9 millimeters by .9 millimeters, or not much larger than a grain of sand. Unreadable by the naked eye, it must be read with a microscope.

In 2007, the world's first nanoscale book was published, although the *Guinness Book of World Records* has not yet recognized it. *Teeny Ted from Turnip Town,* written by Malcolm Douglas Chaplin, is much smaller than *Chameleon.* It measures less than 0.07 millimeters by 0.10 millimeters. Visit http://robertchaplin.ca/pubs/teeny to learn more.

Interested in learning more about miniature books? If so, visit the Miniature Book Society's Web site, http://www.mbs.org.

Earnings

According to a member survey by the Association for Library Collections and Technical Services, acquisitions librarians earn salaries that range from $18,000 to $90,000.

To Be a Successful Acquisitions Librarian, You Should . . .

○ have a love of information

○ have strong computer skills

○ be good at solving problems

○ have excellent communication skills in order to work well with library patrons, vendors, the library director, and other library professionals

○ have business skills to negotiate contracts and licenses for certain materials, such as e-subscriptions

○ be able to manage a budget

Outlook

The U.S. Department of Labor predicts that employment opportunities for librarians, including acquisitions librarians, should be good. Today, libraries offer a wide variety of materials—including books, periodicals, electronic publications and music, CD-ROMs, music, and videos—to patrons, and acquisitions librarians will be needed to assess and acquire these materials. Opportunities will be best at libraries with large collections and a variety of media.

FOR MORE INFO

For career information and a list of accredited schools, contact
American Library Association
50 East Huron Street
Chicago, IL 60611-2729
Tel: 800-545-2433
E-mail: library@ala.org
http://www.ala.org

To learn more about information science careers, contact
The American Society for Information Science & Technology

1320 Fenwick Lane, Suite 510
Silver Spring, MD 20910-3560
Tel: 301-495-0900
E-mail: asis@asis.org
http://www.asis.org

For information on working in a specialized library, contact
Special Libraries Association
331 South Patrick Street
Alexandria, VA 22314-3501
Tel: 703-647-4900
E-mail: sla@sla.org
http://www.sla.org

Archivists

What Archivists Do

Archivists analyze manuscripts, blueprints, photographs, maps, and legal documents and determine which items should be saved and stored. They make records and prepare reference aids, such as indexes, descriptions, and bibliographies. These reference aids help researchers find information in libraries and museums.

Archivists decide if written records should be preserved in their original form, on microfilm, or on computer files. Since very old documents can easily be damaged, it is necessary to copy them in some way so that researchers can still consult them without destroying the originals. Archivists know how to handle and store paper and other materials so they remain undamaged. They also have to know how to repair any damage already done to old documents.

To Be a Successful Archivist, You Should . . .

- ○ have excellent research and organizational skills
- ○ be comfortable working with rare and fragile materials
- ○ be able to respect the privacy of archives, which may be closed to the general public or available only to specific users
- ○ have strong communication skills, in order to explain research methods and the policies and procedures of your organization
- ○ be able to lift or carry large objects

EXPLORING

○ Familiarize yourself with archivist lingo. Visit http://www.archivists. org/glossary/index.asp for a comprehensive glossary of terms.

○ Keep your own family archive. Collect letters; special awards; photographs; birth, marriage, and death certificates; and any other documents that provide facts about your family.

○ See if a professional archival or historical association offers special student memberships or mentoring opportunities.

○ Use archives for your own research. Since institutions may limit access to their collections, be sure to contact the organization about your project before you make the trip.

○ Getting to know an archivist can give you a good sense of the field and the specific duties of the professional archivist.

○ Obtain part-time or volunteer positions in archives, historical societies, or libraries. Many museums and cultural centers train volunteer guides (who are called "docents") to give tours of their institutions.

Archivists work for government agencies, corporations, universities, and museums. When a customer needs information, archivists, like librarians, must be able to quickly locate the correct documents using written or computerized records. They are extremely organized and pay close attention to details. Most archival work is quiet and solitary, but some archivists conduct tours and teach classes and workshops on history or document preservation.

Archivists may have assistants who help them with the sorting and indexing of archival collections. At a university library, undergraduate or graduate students usually act as archival assistants. Small community historical societies may rely on trained volunteers to assist the archivist.

Depending on the size of the employer, archivists may perform many or few administrative duties. They might prepare budgets, represent the institution at scientific or association conferences, solicit support for the institution, and interview and hire personnel. In addition, archivists may plan or participate in special research projects and write articles for scientific journals.

Education and Training

English, history, foreign language, science, and mathematics are important subjects to take in high school. If you have a special interest in a specific kind of archival work, such as medical history, you should take science courses such as anatomy, biology, and chemistry.

Archivists usually need at least a master's degree in history or a related field. For some archivist jobs, you will need a second master's degree in library and information science. Some positions require a doctoral degree as well. After you earn a bachelor's degree, you may work as an assistant in a museum or library while you complete your education.

An archivist displays a page of the Texas Declaration of Independence. (Harry Cabluck, AP Photo)

Earnings

Salaries for archivists vary considerably by institution and may depend on education and experience. The median salary for all archivists was $40,730 in 2006, according to the U.S. Department of Labor. Salaries ranged from less than $23,890 to more than $73,060. Archivists employed by the federal government

Mean Annual Earnings by Industry, 2006

Federal Government	$72,700
Local Government	$43,250
Colleges, Universities, and Professional Schools	$42,880
State Government	$41,730
Museums, Historical Sites, and Similar Institutions	$39,130

Source: U.S. Department of Labor

Archives on the Web

Many archivists are working to make archival collections available digitally so people can have quick and easy access to records from around the world. Below is a small sample of archival collections that are available, in whole or in part, on the Web.

Archives of African American Music and Culture
http://www.indiana.edu/~aaamc

Berkeley Digital Library
http://sunsite.berkeley.edu/Collections

Glenbow Archives
http://www.glenbow.org/collections/archives

The Library of Congress
http://lcweb.loc.gov/exhibits

The National Security Archive
http://www.gwu.edu/~nsarchiv

The Rutgers Oral History Archives
http://oralhistory.rutgers.edu

Smithsonian Archives of American Art
http://www.aaa.si.edu

The U.S. National Archives and Records Administration
http://www.archives.gov

Vanderbilt University Television News Archive
http://tvnews.vanderbilt.edu

or by large museums generally earn more than those working for small organizations. The mean annual salary for archivists working for the federal government was $72,700 in 2006. Those working in museums or historical sites earned a mean salary of $39,130.

Outlook

Job opportunities for archivists are expected to increase about as fast as the average. Jobs are expected to increase as more corporations and private organizations establish an archival history. Archivists will also be needed to fill positions left vacant by retirees and archivists who leave the occupation. On the other hand, budget cuts in educational institutions, museums, and cultural centers can reduce demand for archivists.

Qualified job applicants outnumber the archivist positions available, so there is a high level of competition for jobs. Candidates with specialized training, such as a master's degree in history and in library science, will have better opportunities. A doctorate in history or a related field can

FOR MORE INFO

For information on careers and certification, contact

Academy of Certified Archivists
90 State Street, Suite 1009
Albany, NY 12207-1710
Tel: 518-463-8644
E-mail: aca@caphill.com
http://www.certifiedarchivists.org

For information about archival programs, activities, and publications in North America, contact

American Institute for Conservation of Historic & Artistic Works
1156 15th Street NW, Suite 320
Washington, DC 20005-1714
Tel: 202-452-9545
E-mail: info@aic-faic.org
http://aic.stanford.edu

For information on working with film, television, video, and digital formats, contact

The Association of Moving Image Archivists
1313 North Vine Street
Hollywood, CA 90028-8107
Tel: 323-463-1500
E-mail: amia@amianet.org
http://amianet.org

For a list of educational programs and to read "So You Want to Be an Archivist: An Overview of the Archival Profession," visit the SAA's Web site

Society of American Archivists (SAA)
527 South Wells Street, Fifth Floor
Chicago, IL 60607-3928
Tel: 312-922-0140
E-mail: info@archivists.org
http://www.archivists.org

also benefit job seekers. In addition, those with related work or volunteer experience are in a better position to find full-time employment. Technology is changing the way archival work is conducted. As a result, individuals with extensive knowledge of computers are likely to advance more quickly than an archivist with little desire to learn.

Overall, there will always be positions available for archivists, but the aspiring archivist may need to be creative, flexible, and determined in forging a career path.

Book Conservators

What Book Conservators Do

Book conservators treat the bindings and pages of books to help preserve them for the future. They repair books that have been damaged by misuse, accident, pests, or normal wear and tear.

Book conservators examine books in order to judge how badly they are damaged and to decide how to fix them. They have to consider the book's history: A book bound by hand in Italy in 1600 will be repaired in a different way than a volume bound by machine in 1980.

When repairing a ripped sheet, book conservators use acid-free glue or a special acid-free book tape. High levels of acid in

Words to Learn

bookblock the paper contents of the book, not including the cover

case the outside cover of a book, usually made of two boards covered in cloth and paper

endpapers the first and last leaves of the bookblock, often made of colored or patterned paper

fore-edge the front edge of the book, so named because in early days books were shelved with the spine to the back of the shelf

head the top edge of the book

leaf a single sheet of paper in a book (two pages)

page one side of a leaf

spine the back edge of the book

squares the part of the case boards that overlap the bookblock at the head, tail, and fore-edge to protect the edges of the paper

tail the bottom edge of a book

EXPLORING

○ Learn all you can about how books are made. Study the history of books and binding.

○ Try making a simple, hand-bound book to use as a journal or photo album. There are many "how to" bookbinding guides, such as *Basic Bookbinding,* by A. W. Lewis; *Hand Bookbinding: A Manual of Instruction,* by Aldren A. Watson; *ABC of Bookbinding: An Illustrated Glossary of Terms for Collectors and Conservators,* by Jane Greenfield; and *Making Books by Hand: A Step-by-Step Guide*, by Mary McCarthy and Phillip Manna.

○ Contact the conservation or preservation department at your local library. They may offer tours of their facilities or workshops on the proper care of books.

○ Community colleges, art museums, or community centers may have weekend or evening classes in bookbinding arts.

○ Ask your school counselor or librarian to help arrange an information interview with a book conservator.

papers and materials make books wear out faster. All materials that a conservator uses are acid free so they will last for many years.

If a book is falling out of its cover, conservators may need to glue the cover back on. If the cover is broken, the book will need a new cover. Conservators measure out the board and book cloth, cut materials to size, and glue the cloth onto the board. They size the bookblock (the book's pages), glue them, and set them in the cover. Conservators make sure that all materials are fitted in properly before the glue is dry.

For some rare books, a conservator may choose to make a box to house the book rather than repair a broken spine. Sometimes it's better to simply stop the damage instead of trying to repair it.

Sometimes bugs can cause damage by eating through paper, glue, and binding. Conservators make sure that all the bugs are dead or take the books to a special place where chemical treatments will kill the mites or other bugs before the volumes are repaired.

Conservators work in libraries, museums, conservation organizations, large corporations, universities, and government agencies.

Education and Training

High school courses in history, literature, art, foreign languages, chemistry, and mathematics will all help you build a strong background for book conservation.

Book conservators need to have thorough knowledge of bookbinding arts and papers. It is recommended that you earn a bachelor's degree, even though it is not required. A degree in art, art history, or fine arts may help you get into a book conservation apprenticeship or internship program. After earning a bachelor's degree, you may wish to attend library school to earn a master's degree in library science.

Earnings

It is difficult to say how much the average book conservator makes, since many conservators work part time, are

It's a Fact

○ The ancestor of the modern book was the codex, invented in the second century. It was a collection of handwritten sheets fastened together at one edge. Before the codex, parchment was cut into rectangles and sewn together into long sheets that were made into rolls.

○ The printing of books first developed in the Far East, where the Chinese invented block printing. Each page was printed from a single carved wooden block.

○ By the middle of the thirteenth century, paper began to replace parchment in bookmaking.

○ In about 1450, printing with movable type was developed; by the end of the fifteenth century, some 15 to 20 million copies of books had been printed.

○ Books printed before 1501 are called *incunabula*, a Latin word meaning "cradle books."

How to Conserve Books

Do the following to take care of books:

○ Keep books out of the sun. Ultraviolet rays can discolor materials and increase deterioration.

○ Don't throw books around. Treat them with respect.

○ Never bend pages to mark your place. Use a bookmark.

○ Keep food and drinks away from books you are reading. Crumbs left in books can invite pests.

○ Don't place books open face down on a surface. This can break the binding.

○ Don't use books as coasters. Find something else to hold your drink!

○ If you accidentally damage a library book, tell the librarian when you return it so it can be repaired before further damage occurs.

self-employed, or have positions that involve other duties as well. The salary range for book conservators likely falls within the range the U.S. Department of Labor reports for all conservators, archivists, and other museum workers. In 2006, this group of professionals had a median annual income of $34,340. Salaries ranged from less than $20,600 to more than $61,270 per year.

Often the size of the employer affects how much a conservator earns, with larger employers able to pay more. In addition, book conservators in major metropolitan areas generally earn more than those in small cities, and those with more skills also command higher salaries.

Outlook

Employment for book conservators will grow about as fast as the average. The U.S. Department of Labor notes that while the outlook for conservators in general is favorable, there is strong competition for jobs. Book conservators who are graduates of conservation programs and are willing to relocate should have the best opportunities for employment. Those who can use their conservation skills in tandem with other abilities may also find more job openings. Book conservators with artistic talents, for instance, could bring their conservation skills to an exhibition program at an art museum. Conservators who enjoy public contact could use their practical experience to teach classes in conservation techniques.

FOR MORE INFO

For information about conservation programs, activities, and publications, contact
American Institute for Conservation of Historic & Artistic Works
1156 15th Street NW, Suite 320
Washington, DC 20005-1714
Tel: 202-452-9545
E-mail: info@aic-faic.org
http://aic.stanford.edu

For information on book conservation, contact
Guild of Book Workers
521 Fifth Avenue
New York, NY 10175-0083
http://palimpsest.stanford.edu/byorg/gbw

For information on conservation opportunities in Canada, contact

Canadian Conservation Institute
1030 Innes Road
Ottawa, ON K1A 0M5 Canada
Tel: 613-998-3721
http://www.pch.gc.ca/cci-icc

For information about preservation methods, services, and opportunities, contact the following organization
The Library of Congress Preservation Directorate
http://lcweb.loc.gov/preserv

For a wealth of information about conservation topics, check out this project of the Preservation Department of Stanford University Libraries and Academic Information Resources
Conservation OnLine
http://palimpsest.stanford.edu

Children's Librarians

What Children's Librarians Do

Many libraries have special departments that have been created just for children. This library within a library, often called a children's library, houses collections of fiction and nonfiction books, research tools (such as encyclopedias and atlases), computer programs and games, traditional toys and puzzles, and other resources that are suitable for young people. *Children's librarians,* also known as *youth services librarians,* manage the daily operations of this library department. If employed in a school setting, such librarians are called *library media specialists.*

Children's librarians help young library patrons find and choose resources best suited to their needs—whether for school research, personal knowledge, or simply the enjoyment of reading a book or finding a useful or entertaining resource.

The primary responsibility of children's librarians is to maintain and organize the library. One of their most important tasks is selecting and ordering books and other media. This includes fiction and nonfiction books, reference books such as encyclopedias and dictionaries, study guides, maps, periodicals, videos, DVDs, and music. Children's librarians organize

Not a Light Read

You will need to be very strong to read the largest book in the world—*Bhutan: A Visual Odyssey Across the Kingdom,* which is a photographic book about Bhutan, a small country in Asia. The book, which was published in 2003, measures 5 feet x 7 feet, is 112 pages in length, and weighs a whopping 133 pounds! Its paper, if spread out end to end, could cover a football field! Each book costs $2,000 to produce. The book's creator is charging $10,000 for each copy, which will be donated to a charity that builds schools in Cambodia and Bhutan.

Source: The Associated Press

this material so it is easy to find. All new material must be cataloged (usually by computer) by title, author, and subject matter. Children's librarians must regularly inventory their collection to locate lost or overdue books, to identify books that need repairs, or to dispose of old or worn materials.

Children's librarians are teachers as well. They have a strong knowledge of their library's collection so they can easily help students with research questions, or guide them toward a reading selection suited for their grade or reading level. Children's librarians also teach young people how to locate books within the library's collection with the Dewey Decimal system and/or online catalog systems, or how to use computers to do research on the Internet. They also teach visitors how to use library equipment such as audiovisual equipment, copy machines, or computers.

Children's librarians might also arrange and oversee special projects such as story times for toddlers and preschool-age children, holiday parties, puppet shows, summer reading programs and challenges, author visits, and book clubs.

Children's librarians manage, or supervise, other workers. They supervise library technicians and non-professional staff such as clerks, student workers, or volunteers.

EXPLORING

○ Nurture your love of books by reading!
○ Read industry publications, such as *YALS: Young Adult Library Services* (http://www.alaorg/ala/yalsa/yalsa pubs/publications.htm), to learn more about the career.
○ Learn about the Dewey Decimal Classification system so you can navigate a library.
○ Join clubs or find activities that will give you plenty of experience playing and working with children.
○ Volunteer to work in your school library to learn more about this career.
○ Visit Web sites of library associations (see For More Info). Their sites can provide information about education programs and careers.
○ Talk to a children's librarian about his or her career. Ask the following questions: What do you like most and least about your job? Why did you choose a career as a children's librarian? What advice would you give to someone interested in the career?

To Be a Successful Children's Librarian, You Should . . .

- ○ enjoy working with children
- ○ be a good teacher
- ○ have the patience to explain library services and technology to children of different ages and with varied levels of understanding
- ○ be a good problem solver
- ○ be detail oriented
- ○ love managing information
- ○ be willing to continue to learn throughout your career

Children's librarians should enjoy working with young people of varying ages and levels of understanding. (Bob Daemmrich, The Image Works)

Education and Training

In high school, take history, math, English, speech, and computer science to prepare for college.

If you plan to work as a children's librarian in a public library, you will need a master's degree in library science. You should attend a library program that is accredited by the American Library Association (ALA). If you would like to work in a school setting, you can pursue either a master's degree in library science from an ALA-accredited program or a master's degree with a specialty in school library media from a school that is accredited by the National Council for Accreditation of Teacher Education (http://www.ncate.org).

Earnings

Salaries for children's librarians depend on such factors as the size, location, and type of library; the responsibilities of the position; and the amount of experience the librarian has. According to the U.S. Department of Labor, median annual earnings of all librarians were $49,060 in 2006. Salaries ranged from less than $30,930 to more than $74,670. Librarians working in elementary and secondary school earned a mean annual salary of $52,250. Librarians employed by local government earned a mean annual salary of $46,470.

Outlook

The U.S. Department of Labor predicts good employment opportunities for librarians, including children's librarians. This specialty is a popular choice for many aspiring librarians, which means that competition for the best jobs will remain strong over the next decade. Children's librarians who are willing to take lower-paying positions in rural areas will have the best employment prospects.

FOR MORE INFO

For career information and a list of accredited schools, contact
American Library Association
50 East Huron Street
Chicago, IL 60611-2729
Tel: 800-545-2433
E-mail: library@ala.org
http://www.ala.org

For information on a career as a children's librarian, contact
Association for Library Service to Children
50 East Huron Street
Chicago, IL 60611-2729
Tel: 800-545-2433, ext. 2163
E-mail: alsc@ala.org
http://www.ala.org/ala/alsc/alsc.htm

For career information, contact
Young Adult Library Services Association
50 East Huron Street
Chicago, IL 60611-2729
Tel: 800-545-2433, ext. 4390
E-mail: yalsa@ala.org
http://www.ala.org/yalsa

College Professors, Library Science

What College Professors, Library Science Do

College and university library science faculty instruct students at colleges and universities. Library science professors have three main responsibilities: teaching, advising, and conducting research. Teaching is the most important. Library science professors give lectures, lead discussions, give exams, and assign textbook reading and term papers. They may spend fewer than 10 hours a week in the classroom, but they spend many hours

Library Firsts

- The first library was established in Sumeria around 2700 BC.
- The Alexandria Library was the first public library in the world. It was established in Egypt about 300 BC.
- The Library Company of Philadelphia was the first library in the American colonies that was created for the average person (libraries before this were open only to wealthy people). Benjamin Franklin and a group of friends established it in 1731.
- The first public library, supported from public funds and open to all readers, was established in Boston in 1854.
- In 1887, the first library school—the School of Library Economy—was established at Columbia University in New York by Melvil Dewey, the founder of the Dewey Decimal Classification system.
- In 1926, the first library graduate school was established at the University of Chicago. The university also offered the first doctoral program in library studies.
- In 1995, the University of Michigan established the first Internet public library.

preparing lectures and lesson plans, grading papers and exams, and preparing grade reports. They also meet with students individually outside of class to guide them in the course and keep them updated about their progress.

Some library science faculty members also work as undergraduate student advisers, helping students decide which courses to take, informing them of requirements for their majors, and directing them toward scholarships and other financial aid. They may also help students adjust to college life and guide them through difficult problems.

Many library science professors conduct research in their field and publish the results in textbooks and journals (such as *American Libraries, Computers in Libraries,* and *School Library Journal).* They attend conferences and present research findings to professors from other universities. They employ graduate students as assistants both in research projects and in teaching.

Distance learning programs are an increasingly popular option for library science students. They give library science professors the opportunity to teach students who are in a variety of locations simultaneously. (To view a good example of an online library science program, visit http://www.lis.uiuc. edu/programs/leep.) Computers, the Internet, e-mail, and video conferencing are some of the technology tools that allow library science professors and students to communicate in "real time" in a virtual classroom setting. Meetings may be scheduled during the same time as traditional classes or during evenings and weekends. Library science professors who do this work are sometimes known as *extension work instructors, correspondence instructors,* or *distance learning instructors.* They may teach online courses in addition to other classes or may do distance learning as their major teaching responsibility.

The *junior college library instructor* has many of the same kinds of responsibilities as does the teacher in a college or university that offers undergraduate and graduate degrees. Because junior colleges offer only a two-year program, professors there teach

EXPLORING

○ Talk to your teachers about their careers and their education.

○ Visit the Web sites of college library science programs. Look at course catalogs and read about the faculty members and the courses they teach. You might consider e-mailing a library professor with questions about the field. The American Library Association provides a list of accredited schools at its Web site, http://www.ala.org.

○ Volunteer with a community center, day care center, or summer camp to get teaching experience.

only undergraduates. These instructors typically teach library, media, and information science to students who are interested in becoming library assistants and technicians.

Education and Training

During your middle school and high school years, you should concentrate on a college-preparatory program. Take courses in English, science, foreign languages, history, math, and government. In addition, you should take courses in speech to get a sense of what it will be like to lecture to a group of students. Your school's debate team can also help you develop public speaking skills, along with research skills.

At least one advanced degree in library and information science is

To Be a Successful College Library Science Professor, You Should . . .

○ be an expert in library and information science

○ enjoy reading, writing, and researching

○ be self-confident

○ have leadership abilities

○ be able to communicate your thoughts and ideas to students and colleagues

○ have good people skills in order to interact with students, administrators, and other faculty members

○ be willing to continue to learn throughout your career

required to be a library science professor in a college or university. The master's degree is considered the minimum standard, and graduate work beyond the master's is usually desirable. If you hope to advance in academic rank above instructor, most institutions require a doctorate.

You may find employment in a junior college with only a master's degree. Advancement in responsibility and in salary, however, is more likely to come if you have earned a doctorate.

Typical Library Science Courses

- ○ History of Libraries
- ○ Introduction to Library Science
- ○ Literature and Resources for Children
- ○ Literature and Resources for Young Adults
- ○ Literature and Resources for Adults
- ○ Literature and Resources for Special Libraries
- ○ Introduction to Network Systems
- ○ Search Engines and Information Retrieval Systems
- ○ Understanding Multimedia Information: Concepts and Practices
- ○ Reference and Information Services
- ○ Administration and Management of Libraries and Information Centers
- ○ Cataloging and Classification
- ○ Bibliography
- ○ Indexing and Abstracting
- ○ Information Ethics
- ○ Legal Issues in Library and Information Science
- ○ Digital Libraries
- ○ Electronic Records Management
- ○ Web Technologies and Techniques
- ○ Emerging Technologies

FOR MORE INFO

To read about the issues affecting college professors, contact the following organizations

American Association of University Professors
1012 14th Street NW, Suite 500
Washington, DC 20005-3406
Tel: 202-737-5900
E-mail: aaup@aaup.org
http://www.aaup.org

American Federation of Teachers
555 New Jersey Avenue NW
Washington, DC 20001-2029
Tel: 202-879-4400
E-mail: online@aft.org
http://www.aft.org

For information on careers in library education, contact
Association for Library and Information Science Education
65 East Wacker Place, Suite 1900
Chicago, IL 60601-7246
Tel: 312-795-0996
E-mail: contact@alise.org
http://www.alise.org

Earnings

Earnings vary by the size of the school, the type of school (public or private, for example), and the level of position the library science educator holds. According to the U.S. Department of Labor, in 2006, the median salary for library science educators was $54,570. Salaries ranged from less than $33,120 to more than $87,430. Those with the highest earnings tend to be senior faculty; those with the lowest, graduate assistants.

Outlook

Opportunities for library science educators should be strong over the next decade. There are three main factors behind this prediction. First, the American Library Association predicts a shortage of librarians during the next decade. Second, there will be increased demand for library science educators as existing educators retire. (According to the Association for Library and Information Science Education, 37.1 percent of library science professors were 55 or older in 2003). Finally, continued growth in technology and information-gathering resources will create a need for more library professionals. However, competition for full-time, tenure-track positions at four-year schools will be very strong. Library science professionals with the highest education will have the best opportunities in coming years.

Corporate Librarians

What Corporate Librarians Do

Public libraries and schools are not the only places librarians work. Today many librarians work for various companies and institutions throughout the United States, such as large corporations, private businesses, law firms, hospitals and medical interest companies, museums, colleges, associations, and the government. These librarians are called *corporate librarians,* but they are sometimes referred to as *special librarians, information specialists,* or *research librarians.*

Corporate librarians gather information of interest to their particular company. This material includes reference books, articles, reports, conferences, films and videos, and many other resources. This data is then organized, cataloged, and indexed into a working database easily accessible by the employees of the company.

The 10 Best Companies to Work for in 2007

Corporate librarians work for businesses of all kinds. *Forbes* magazine rated the following companies as the best places to work in 2007. All offer employment opportunities for corporate librarians and other information science professionals.

1. Google
2. Genentech
3. Wegmans Food Markets
4. The Container Store
5. Whole Foods Market
6. Network Appliance
7. S. C. Johnson & Son
8. The Boston Consulting Group
9. Methodist Hospital System
10. W. L. Gore & Associates

Source: *Forbes* magazine

EXPLORING

- Visit your school or local library to learn as much as you can about the daily operations of a library.
- Volunteer to work in your school library to learn more about this career.
- Join a library club at your school. If one doesn't exist, you could start your own.
- Library associations dealing with a particular industry, such as the American Association of Law Libraries or the Medical Library Association (see For More Info), can provide career insight and access to online discussion groups.
- Ask your librarian to talk with you about the career. Perhaps he or she could recommend a corporate librarian whom you could contact for more information.

Corporate librarians help other workers with a project or presentation by conducting research, verifying facts, or locating certain photos or film. At times, they may be asked to write reports, gather data, or do a background search on a particular topic. Much of their work is connected to the Internet, so corporate librarians must be experts in computers and technology. They may also teach employees how to use new computer equipment or software. Corporate librarians must also keep current with trends and developments concerning their specific industries. Corporate librarians save company time, energy, and resources.

The daily duties of a corporate librarian depend on where he or she works. For example, a research librarian for a television network may be asked to provide background research or locate past film footage for a feature documentary. A pharmaceutical company may rely on an information specialist to compile data to help in the launch of a new drug. Government agencies or private organizations may rely on a special librarian to cull and archive decades of work or reports and other documents.

Three of the most popular types of corporate librarians are medical librarians, law librarians, and advertising librarians.

Education and Training

Take a college-preparatory course load in high school to prepare for this career. Take classes in history, English, and speech, as well as business classes such as marketing and finance. Since corporate librarians rely on computers and the Internet to do their work, it is a good idea to take computer classes and fine-tune your Internet research skills. If you plan on working in a particular specialty, then it would be wise to take related classes. For example, if you'd like to work as a librarian at the American Medical Association, you should take classes in biology, chemistry, and anatomy and physiology.

To work as a corporate librarian, you will need a master in library science (MLS) or master of library information science (MLIS). Schools offering this degree can be found throughout the United States, but programs accredited by the American Library Association (ALA) carry the most weight with prospective employers. There are more than 55 ALA-accredited programs available.

Many specialized librarians also earn a bachelor's degree that is complementary to their field. For example, corporate librarians working for financial institutions may have an undergraduate degree in business administration or finance. Those employed by advertising agencies may have an undergraduate degree in advertising. Medical librarians may have an educational background in

To Be a Successful Corporate Librarian, You Should . . .

○ be very organized

○ be very skilled with computers, the Internet, and related technologies

○ have strong communication skills

○ be a good researcher

○ be able to work under tight deadlines

○ have a strong background in your particular specialty; for example, an advertising librarian should have knowledge of the advertising industry and be familiar with industry companies, publications, lingo, and trends

FOR MORE INFO

For career information and a list of accredited schools, contact

American Library Association
50 East Huron Street
Chicago, IL 60611-2729
Tel: 800-545-2433
E-mail: library@ala.org
http://www.ala.org

To learn more about information science careers, contact

The American Society for Information Science & Technology
1320 Fenwick Lane, Suite 510
Silver Spring, MD 20910-3560
Tel: 301-495-0900
E-mail: asis@asis.org
http://www.asis.org

For information on working in a specialized library, contact

Special Libraries Association
331 South Patrick Street
Alexandria, VA 22314-3501
Tel: 703-647-4900
E-mail: sla@sla.org
http://www.sla.org

science or work experience in the health-care industry.

Some large law firms expect their corporate librarians to have a law degree in addition to an MLS/MLIS. In fact, according to the American Association of Law Libraries, nearly 30 percent of all law librarians have a law degree. Some schools now offer a combined JD/MLS program, lasting about four years.

Earnings

Salaries for corporate librarians vary by type of employer, geographic region, and the experience of the librarian. Corporate librarians earned average salaries of $60,000 to $65,000 in 2003, according to the outplacement firm Challenger, Gray & Christmas. The Special Libraries Association reports that special librarians, including corporate librarians, earned salaries that ranged from less than $40,000 to more than $100,000 in 2006.

Outlook

Challenger, Gray & Christmas recently named the career of corporate librarian as a hot job for the future. Since corporate librarians work in many different sectors of the economy, job prospects will vary based on the overall economic health of the industry in which the corporate librarian is employed. Currently, the strongest industries for corporate librarians are pharmaceuticals and law and medical organizations.

Database Specialists

What Database Specialists Do

The collection of information stored in a computer is called a database. *Database specialists* set up and maintain databases. They purchase computer equipment and create computer programs that collect, analyze, store, and send information. They work for utility companies, stores, investment companies, insurance companies, publishing firms, telecommunications firms, and all branches of government.

Some database specialists determine the type of computer system their company needs. Together with company officials they decide what type of hardware and software will be required to set up a certain type of database. Then a *database design analyst* writes a proposal that states the company's needs, the type of equipment that will meet those needs, and how much the equipment will cost.

Database managers and *administrators* decide how to organize and store the information in the database. They create a computer program or a series of programs and train employees to enter information into computers.

Computer programs sometimes crash, or work improperly. Database specialists make sure that a backup copy of the program and the database is available in case of a crash. Specialists are also responsible for protecting the database from people or organizations that are not supposed to see it.

EXPLORING

○ Read books and magazines about databases and database management.

○ The Association for Computing Machinery has a Special Interest Group on Management of Data (SIGMOD). The Resources page of SIGMOD's Web site (http://www.sigmod.org) provides videos of people who work with databases and an index of public domain database software that you may want to check out.

○ Volunteer to work on databases at your school, religious institution, or local charity.

○ Join a computer club. School computer clubs offer a good way to learn about computers and meet others interested in the field.

○ Ask your guidance counselor or computer teacher to arrange for a database specialist to speak to your class at school or to arrange for a field trip to a company so your class can see database specialists at work.

Very large companies may have many databases. Sometimes it is necessary for these databases to share information. Database managers see to it that these different databases can communicate with each other, even if they are located in different parts of the country.

Education and Training

If you are interested in becoming a database specialist, you should take as many computer courses as possible. In addition, you should study mathematics, accounting, science, English, and communications.

An associate's degree in a computer-related technology is required for entry-level database administrators. You need a bachelor's degree in computer science or business administration for advanced positions. Those with a master's degree will have even greater opportunities.

Earnings

According to the U.S. Department of Labor, database specialists earned an average of $64,670 in 2006. Salaries ranged from less than $37,350 to more than $103,010. Earnings vary with the size, type, and location of the organization as well as a person's experience, education, and job responsibilities. Database administrators and consultants working for major computer companies usually earn the highest salaries.

To Be a Successful Database Specialist, You Should . . .

○ have excellent computer skills

○ be a strong logical and analytical thinker

○ be organized

○ be able to analyze large amounts of information quickly

○ have strong communication skills

○ be willing to pursue continuing education throughout your career

Outlook

The use of computers and database systems in almost all business settings creates great opportunities for well-qualified database personnel. The career of database specialist is predicted by the U.S. Department of Labor to be among the fastest growing occupations through the next decade.

FOR MORE INFO

To learn more about information science careers, contact

The American Society for Information Science & Technology
1320 Fenwick Lane, Suite 510
Silver Spring, MD 20910-3560
Tel: 301-495-0900
E-mail: asis@asis.org
http://www.asis.org

For information on career opportunities and student chapters, contact

Association of Information Technology Professionals
401 North Michigan Avenue, Suite 2400
Chicago, IL 60611-4267
Tel: 800-224-9371
http://www.aitp.org/index.jsp

Film and Video Librarians

What Film and Video Librarians Do

Libraries are no longer limited to traditional collections of books and periodicals. They now include all forms of media, including music, film, and video. Those in charge of a special department or collection of film and videos are called *film and video librarians,* or *media librarians.* Their duties are similar to that of reference librarians, except they know everything there is to know about film and video in all formats. Film and video librarians work in all types of libraries: public, government, corporate or special, and in school libraries.

Film and video librarians maintain their library's collection of film and video. They catalog the items into the library's database according to their title or subject matter, or by actors/actresses and director. To prepare each film or video for circulation, each must be put in a protective covering or case, labeled with the library's name and address, and given a barcode (a method to electronically track each film or video) and checkout card. Film and video librarians also store (known as archiving) and preserve existing material. In addition, they may be responsible for purchasing and maintaining audiovisual equipment.

Where Do They Work?

- ○ public libraries
- ○ school libraries
- ○ corporate libraries
- ○ media centers
- ○ colleges and universities
- ○ film societies
- ○ motion picture studios
- ○ associations
- ○ government agencies

Film and video librarians must make sure that their collection is appropriate for the needs of their library. For example, medical libraries would be interested in films and videos on diseases, treatments, and health-care issues; a civil rights museum would be interested in films and videos about Martin Luther King Jr., Rosa Parks, the 1963 March on Washington, and other topics or individuals related to the civil rights movement; and the library of a women's studies department would be interested in films and videos about famous women (such as Susan B. Anthony, who played a key role in helping U.S. women obtain the right to vote), women's rights, and other related issues.

Film and video librarians at public institutions have the harder task of building a collection that appeals to many different tastes and needs. They have a working knowledge of many different subject areas, including biographies of famous people, historical events, health, theater and the arts, popular culture, anime (a style of animation developed in Japan), and children's interests.

Film and video librarians also hire, train, schedule, and supervise department staff. They write reviews of new materials, compile bibliographies, and give lectures on particular films or videos. They also help students or library patrons find information, answer questions, and instruct people on the proper use of audiovisual equipment.

EXPLORING

○ Take film classes or join a photography club.

○ A part-time job at a local library or your school's media center is a great way to explore this career.

○ What better way to nurture your love of movies than by working at your local video store? Not only will you have access to the newest releases, but you'll also gain familiarity with films in a variety of subject areas.

○ Talk to a film and video librarian about his or her career. Ask the following questions: What are your job duties? What do you like least and most about your job? What advice would you give a young person who is interested in the field?

To Be a Successful Film and Video Librarian, You Should . . .

○ be very knowledgeable about film and video

○ know how to use computers and other technology

○ have strong organizational skills

○ be attentive to detail

○ be able to work well with coworkers and library patrons

○ be willing to learn about new technology throughout your career

A librarian at a museum searches through microfilms. (Troy Talbot, AP Photo)

Education and Training

Take classes in English, history, science, foreign languages, art, computer science, film, and mathematics in high school to prepare for this career. Classes that require you to write numerous research papers will give you good experience in writing and utilizing different library resources. Film and video librarians often give class lectures or hold discussion groups. If you dread speaking in front of a small group, consider taking a speech class or join the debate team to hone your verbal communication skills.

Most, if not all, librarians working in college, corporate, or public libraries have a master's degree in library science (MLS) or a master's degree in information systems (MIS). It is important to have earned an MLS or

MIS from a program that is accredited by the American Library Association. Many film and video librarians have a bachelor's degree in liberal arts and/or extensive experience in film.

Earnings

How much you earn will depend on where you work, the size and type of employer, the amount of experience you have, and your job responsibilities. According to the U.S. Department of Labor, librarians had median annual earnings of $49,060 in 2006. Salaries ranged from less than $30,930 to more than $74,670. Librarians working in colleges and universities earned $53,930 in 2006, and those in elementary and secondary schools earned $52,250. Librarians employed in local government earned $46,470 in 2006. In the federal government, the mean salary for all librarians was $70,060.

FOR MORE INFO

For career information and a list of accredited schools, contact
American Library Association
50 East Huron Street
Chicago, IL 60611-2729
Tel: 800-545-2433
E-mail: library@ala.org
http://www.ala.org

To learn more about information science careers, contact
The American Society for Information Science & Technology
1320 Fenwick Lane, Suite 510
Silver Spring, MD 20910-3560
Tel: 301-495-0900
E-mail: asis@asis.org
http://www.asis.org

This association is a membership organization for media technology centers.
National Association of Media and Technology Centers
PO Box 9844
Cedar Rapids, IA 52409
Tel: 319-654-0608
http://www.namtc.org

For information on working in a specialized library, contact
Special Libraries Association
331 South Patrick Street
Alexandria, VA 22314-3501
Tel: 703-647-4900
E-mail: sla@sla.org
http://www.sla.org

Outlook

The U.S. Department of Labor predicts good employment opportunities for librarians. Opportunities should also be strong for film and video librarians as more and more films and videos are released to educate and entertain the public. As with most careers, film and video librarians with advanced degrees and knowledge of the latest technology will have the best employment prospects.

Information Brokers

What Information Brokers Do

Information brokers, sometimes called *online researchers* or *independent information professionals,* gather information from online databases and services. They research marketing surveys, newspaper articles, business and government statistics, abstracts, and other sources of information and prepare reports and presentations based on their research.

Information brokers primarily use the Internet and online databases, such as Dialog and LexisNexis, to search for information. They also make extensive use of libraries, historical archives, and other print sources. Personal interviews may also be necessary.

Many research projects are marketing based. For example, if a fruit distribution company wants to make figs as popular as apples and oranges, it might hire consultants and researchers to find some basic information about fig consumption. How many people have even eaten a fig? What articles about figs have been published in national magazines? What have been recent annual sales of figs and fig-based treats? What popular recipes include figs?

The legal profession hires information brokers to research cases, statutes,

Research on the Web

Use the following Web sites to help you perform research on the Web:

Ask for Kids
http://www.askforkids.com

The Big 6
http://www.big6.com/kids

Kids and Teens: School Time
http://dmoz.org/Kids_and_Teens/School_Time

KidsClick
http://www.kidsclick.org

Net's Best for Research
http://www.eduplace.com/kids/hme/k_5/netsbest

Yahoo! Kids
http://kids.yahoo.com

EXPLORING

○ On the Internet, experiment with various search engines; each service has slightly different features and capabilities.

○ If you have searched the Internet for information for a research paper, you already have an idea of what online research is like. Keep using Internet tools to perform research.

○ The reference librarians of your school and public library should be happy to introduce you to the various library tools available.

○ Talk with an information broker about his or her career.

and other sources of law; update law library collections; and locate data to support cases, such as finding expert witnesses or researching the history of the development of a defective product that caused personal injury. The health care industry uses information brokers to gather information on drugs, treatments, devices, illnesses, or clinical trials. An information broker who specializes in public records researches personal records (such as birth, death, marriage, adoption, and criminal records), corporations, and property ownership. Other industries that rely on information brokers include banking and finance, government and public policy, and science and technology.

Specific examples of projects assigned to information brokers include research on the market for independent living facilities for senior citizens, the impact of large grocery chains on independent grocery stores, and what rental car companies do with cars after they're past their prime.

Education and Training

In high school, take computer classes that teach word and data processing programs, presentation programs, and how to use Internet search engines. Any class offered by your high school or public library on information retrieval will familiarize you with database searches. English and composition courses will teach you to organize information and write clearly.

It is recommended that you start with a good liberal arts program in a college or university, and then pursue a master's degree either in a subject specialty or in library and information science. Developing expertise in a particular subject will prepare you for a specialty in information brokering.

Because of the rapidly changing technology, brokers need to attend seminars and take courses through such organizations as the Special Libraries Association.

Earnings

Self-employed information brokers' first few years in the business may be lean ones, and they should expect to make as little as $20,000. As with any small business, it takes a few years to develop contacts and establish a reputation for quality work. Independent information brokers usually charge between $45 and $100 an hour, depending on the project. Eventually, an online researcher should be able to make a salary equivalent to that of a full-time special librarian—a 2006 salary survey by the Special Libraries Association puts the national median at $62,000. Some very experienced independent researchers with a number of years of self-employment may make well over $100,000.

To Be a Successful Information Broker, You Should . . .

○ have excellent research skills

○ be a good communicator

○ have strong computer skills

○ be self-motivated to meet deadlines

○ have good record-keeping skills

○ be willing to stay up to date with current events

○ be persistent in order to pursue new clients and sources of information

FOR MORE INFO

For career information and a list of accredited library schools, contact

American Library Association
50 East Huron Street
Chicago, IL 60611-2729
Tel: 800-545-2433
E-mail: library@ala.org
http://www.ala.org

To learn more about the career of information broker, contact

Association of Independent Information Professionals
8550 United Plaza Boulevard, Suite 1001
Baton Rouge, LA 70809-0200
Tel: 225-408-4400
E-mail: info@aiip.org
http://www.aiip.org/index.html

For information on working in a specialized library, contact

Special Libraries Association
331 South Patrick Street
Alexandria, VA 22314-3501
Tel: 703-647-4900
E-mail: sla@sla.org
http://www.sla.org

Information brokers who work full-time for companies earn salaries comparable to other information technology professionals—roughly $36,000 to more than $100,000 annually.

Outlook

Information professionals will continue to find a great deal of work, but growth in the industry is expected to slow because of the increasing number of new information science graduates entering the field. There will be continuing demand for information brokers in marketing, competitive intelligence, legal research, and science and technology.

Law Librarians

What Law Librarians Do

Law librarians are specialized librarians who are experts of legal books, periodicals, documents, digital databases, and other resources. Lawyers, judges, law students, and faculty all rely on law librarians to help them locate information. The duties of law librarians vary across different work environments, but ultimately, public service and the organization of legal materials are the primary responsibilities of law librarians.

In general, law firms and law departments of corporations hire law librarians to maintain their library's collections. Law librarians in a law firm or corporate law department decide what materials to add and weed out, and catalog the contents of the firm's collections. They may create budgets and supervise support staff.

In addition to the tasks already mentioned, *academic law librarians* who work in college or university law libraries may have a stronger focus on teaching than other law librarians. They may work closely with law school professors and teach law school students where to look for specific information and how to use research tools efficiently.

Government law librarians work in government law offices, courts, and government agencies. They manage law-related materials for lawyers, judges, and other government officials.

Where Do They Work?

- college and university law libraries
- libraries of law firms
- law departments of business corporations or other organizations
- government (in prisons and in state, county, and city legal departments or courts)
- vendors of legal information resources

EXPLORING

○ Read as many books and periodicals about law and librarianship as you can.

○ Visit the Web sites of professional associations (including the American Association of Law Libraries) to learn more about career options, educational requirements, and issues affecting the field.

○ Join a library club at your school. If one doesn't exist, you could start your own.

○ Ask your teacher or guidance counselor to help arrange an information interview with a law librarian.

Some law librarians work for outside vendor companies, usually in sales or training. They use their experience and knowledge of how a law library functions to sell and/or train law library staff in products and services that may meet the information needs of law library staff and patrons.

Education and Training

To become a law librarian, you will need to go to college, so it is necessary to take college-preparatory courses while in high school. Classes in civics, government, and history will give you a useful introduction to law. English and computer classes will also help you prepare for learning the skills you will need as a librarian.

Most positions for law librarians require a master of library science (MLS) or master of library and information science (MLIS). The graduate school you choose should be accredited by the American Library Association, as some law libraries do not consider job applicants who attended a nonaccredited school.

Some law librarians earn a law degree (called a juris doctor, or JD) in addition to their MLS. The additional degree may be earned separately, or you may chose to earn both degrees at the same time. There are several schools that offer joint JD/MLS degrees.

Earnings

Factors affecting earnings in this field include the amount of experience the law librarian has, the responsibilities of his or her position, the size and type of law library in which he or she is employed, and geographic location. Law librarians employed in larger cities tend to make more than their counterparts in smaller metropolitan areas. In 2004, the median salary for law librarians was $58,258, according to the Special Libraries Association. Salaries ranged from less than $38,000 to more than $94,359.

Did You Know?

○ The American Association of Law Libraries represents approximately 5,000 law librarians.

○ 85 percent of law librarians have a graduate degree in library science.

○ Almost 30 percent of law librarians also have a juris doctor or bachelor of laws degree.

Source: American Association of Law Libraries

Outlook

The U.S. Department of Labor predicts that employment of lawyers will grow about as fast as the average. This steady growth for lawyers, and the increasing complexity and sheer

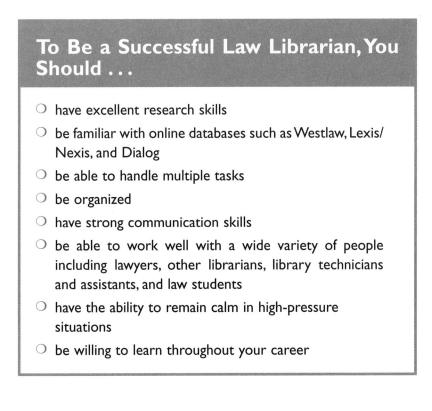

To Be a Successful Law Librarian, You Should . . .

○ have excellent research skills

○ be familiar with online databases such as Westlaw, Lexis/Nexis, and Dialog

○ be able to handle multiple tasks

○ be organized

○ have strong communication skills

○ be able to work well with a wide variety of people including lawyers, other librarians, library technicians and assistants, and law students

○ have the ability to remain calm in high-pressure situations

○ be willing to learn throughout your career

FOR MORE INFO

For information on careers in law librarianship and schools that offer courses or programs in law librarianship, contact
American Association of Law Libraries
53 West Jackson, Suite 940
Chicago, IL 60604-3847
Tel: 312-939-4764
E-mail: aallhq@aall.org
http://www.aallnet.org

For career information and a list of accredited schools, contact
American Library Association
50 East Huron Street
Chicago, IL 60611-2729
Tel: 800-545-2433
E-mail: library@ala.org
http://www.ala.org

For information on working in a specialized library, contact
Special Libraries Association
331 South Patrick Street
Alexandria, VA 22314-3501
Tel: 703-647-4900
E-mail: sla@sla.org
http://www.sla.org

volume of legal materials, suggests that opportunities for law librarians will continue to be strong. Librarians who stay up to date with the latest technology and education in the field will have the best job prospects.

Librarians

What Librarians Do

Librarians are responsible for the books, magazines, newspapers, audiovisual materials, and other sources of information that are found in libraries. They purchase these materials, organize them, and lend them. They also answer questions about the collections in the library and help people find the information they need.

There are many different types of libraries: college and university libraries, public libraries, school library media centers, and libraries containing rare or unique collections.

Public library work is probably the most familiar. Because there are many duties to perform, librarians often specialize

Famous Librarians

Did you know that Laura Bush, wife of George W. Bush, the 43rd president of the United States, was a librarian? She earned a master's of library science from the University of Texas and worked as a public school librarian. Here are some other well-known people who have worked as librarians (with nationalities and more famous career paths in parentheses).

Hector Berlioz (French composer)

Jorge Luis Borges (Argentine writer)

Lewis Carroll (English writer)

Beverly Cleary (American writer)

Benjamin Franklin (American statesman, inventor, scientist, printer)

Johann Wolfgang von Goethe (German writer)

The Brothers Grimm (German writers/publishers)

J. Edgar Hoover (American director of the Federal Bureau of Investigation)

David Hume (English philosopher)

Stanley Kunitz (American writer, editor)

Philip Larkin (English writer)

Archibald MacLeish (American writer)

A librarian (left) *helps a library patron locate information.* (Jeff Greenberg, The Image Works)

in certain areas. *Library directors* are in charge of all the public libraries in a particular system. They supervise the chief librarians who run each of the branch libraries or the individual departments in large branch libraries.

In large branch libraries, the *chief librarians* supervise those who head the various departments such as acquisitions, cataloging, and reference. *Acquisitions librarians* buy books and other materials for the library. *Cataloging librarians* organize materials by subject matter. They give each item a classification number and prepare the cards or computer records that will help users find items. *Reference librarians* help readers find information in encyclopedias, almanacs, online computer databases, and other sources. *Children's librarians* help children select materials they would enjoy. They show children how to use the library, and organize special events such as story hours. *Bookmobile librarians* bring library services to rural and hard-to-reach places.

Not all librarians work in public libraries. Those who work in school library media centers also teach classes in library use. They help students with their assignments and select materials that teachers can use in the classroom.

Some librarians work in special libraries, such as medical libraries. They purchase and organize materials of interest to a particular group of people—in this case, researchers, physicians, nurses, and medical assistants. Other special research libraries serve the science, business, engineering, and legal communities.

Education and Training

If you want to become a librarian, you should take classes in history, English, computers, and foreign languages in high school. All of these courses will help you learn how to do research in a library. They also will help you prepare for college.

After high school, you will need to earn a bachelor's degree, usually in the liberal arts. After college, you should attend a school accredited by the American Library Association and earn a master's in library science (MLS) or master's in library and information science (MLIS). If you hope to advance to higher administrative levels in a library, you will need to earn a doctoral degree (known as a Ph.D.) in library science or in a specialized subject area. Most states require that school library media specialists, who work in grade school and high school libraries, have a teacher's certificate in addition to a master's degree in library science.

EXPLORING

○ Talk to your school or community librarian. He or she can give you a good idea of what goes on behind the scenes.

○ Some schools may have library clubs you can join to learn about library work. Or consider starting your own library club.

○ You might be able to work as an assistant in the school library or media center. You can check materials in and out at the circulation desk, shelve returned books, or type title, subject, and author information in computer records.

Earnings

Salaries vary according to the location, size, and type of library and the amount of education and experience the librarian has. According to the U.S. Department of Labor, median annual

Library Employment

Type of Library	Number of Librarians	Number of Other Paid Staff
School Libraries	66,471	99,557
Public Libraries	45,037	90,977
Academic Libraries	25,936	68,149

Source: American Library Association

A Division for Every Interest

The American Library Association (ALA), the oldest and largest library association in the world, has 11 membership units, called divisions. These focus on particular types of library services or libraries. The ALA divisions include:

- American Association of School Librarians
- Association for Library Collections & Technical Services
- Association for Library Service to Children
- Association for Library Trustees and Advocates
- Association of College & Research Libraries
- Association of Specialized and Cooperative Library Agencies
- Library Administration and Management Association
- Library & Information Technology Association
- Public Library Association
- Reference and User Services Association
- Young Adult Library Services Association

earnings of librarians in 2006 were $49,060. Salaries ranged from less than $30,930 to more than $74,670. Librarians working in elementary and secondary schools earned $52,250, and those in colleges and universities earned $53,930.

Outlook

The U.S. Department of Labor predicts that employment for librarians will grow more slowly than the average. Many librarians are being replaced with library technicians who have less education and experience, and make less money. Librarians with science, law, business, and engineering backgrounds will have better luck in finding a job. The outlook is better for those who speak a second language, have a thorough knowledge of computers, or have advanced degrees in specialized subject areas.

Employment opportunities will be best in nontraditional library settings, such as information brokers, private corporations, and consulting firms.

Employment opportunities will also arise for librarians who have a background in information science and library automation. The rapidly expanding field of information management has created a demand for qualified people to set up and maintain information systems for private industry and consulting firms. Many companies are also establishing in-house reference libraries to assist in research work. Some have developed full lending library systems for employees.

FOR MORE INFO

To learn more about information science careers, contact
The American Society for Information Science & Technology
1320 Fenwick Lane, Suite 510
Silver Spring, MD 20910-3560
Tel: 301-495-0900
E-mail: asis@asis.org
http://www.asis.org

For information on working in a specialized library, contact
Special Libraries Association
331 South Patrick Street
Alexandria, VA 22314-3501
Tel: 703-647-4900
E-mail: sla@sla.org
http://www.sla.org

For information on library careers in Canada, contact
Canadian Library Association
328 Frank Street
Ottawa, ON K2P 0X8 Canada
Tel: 613-232-9625
E-mail: info@cla.ca
http://www.cla.ca

Library Assistants

What Library Assistants Do

From sorting to stacking to swiping, *library assistants* keep books, periodicals, and other resource materials organized and easily accessible. Don't let the job title fool you; these professionals are critical in helping libraries, media centers, research facilities, and other information-based organizations run smoothly and effectively.

Library assistants help library directors, librarians, research assistants, and other library staff organize materials and help the public find the information they need. They may work in the checkout area, scanning books in and out of the library. They also may work among the shelves, pushing carts of returned and misshelved books and other material and returning items to their proper place. They may specialize in electronic media, helping to organize CD-ROMs, microfiches, and DVDs so they are accessible to library patrons.

In addition to checking materials in and out of the library, assistants also prepare and repair books so that they are suitable for lending. They may affix barcodes to materials and also place protective book covers—usually made of a thin, but durable plastic—on all books and periodicals. Compact discs, records, and other irregularly sized

Where Do They Work?

Library assistants hold approximately 109,000 jobs in the United States. They work in:
- public libraries
- school libraries
- library media centers
- college or university libraries
- nonprofit organizations
- government agencies
- research libraries
- corporate libraries
- medical libraries
- law libraries
- other special libraries

items must also be prepared for the shelves and protected from the wear and tear that comes with constant handling.

Assistants working in circulation collect fines for overdue items. They scan the patron's library card to make sure no items are overdue and then assign new materials to the card. Most modern libraries have computer systems that track books' due dates to help library assistants locate individuals with overdue items. Library assistants mail notices to people who rack up large fines and collect smaller fines from patrons in person. These duties are crucial to a library's financial well-being and ability to invest in more books and to care for those already in the collection.

All library assistants report to head and departmental librarians. All tasks are delegated to the assistants by these supervisors.

EXPLORING

○ Spend as much time as possible in your school or public library. Take notice of how materials are organized and handled from drop-off to pickup. Just using your own library for school projects or scanning the aisles for new books will increase your knowledge of how libraries are organized.

○ Try to get a job working part time in your school or public library as an assistant. Even just working on a volunteer basis will give you experiences.

○ The American Library Association and other professional organizations (see For More Info) offer information on careers, education, and student memberships. Be sure to explore these associations.

Education and Training

Library assistants need strong English, history, speech, and even foreign language skills, so while in high school concentrate on the humanities. If you are interested in working in a special library such as a medical library, take classes in that specialty. Learning how to use a computer and conduct basic research in a library is essential.

While little college training is required for an assistant job, the position is often a stepping-stone to a higher library position. If this is your goal, you will need to work

A library assistant uses a computer database to check the status of a book. (Jeff Greenberg, The Image Works)

toward a master's degree in library science. The assistant job will provide wonderful on-the-job training. This, coupled with education in the communications, writing, research methods, collection organization, and customer service, as well as maintenance and conservation, will put you in a great position to land a librarian position.

Earnings

Your salary will depend on such factors as your experience, your job responsibilities, and the location, size, and type of your employer. According to the U.S. Department of Labor, the median annual salary of library assistants was $21,640 in

To Be a Successful Library Assistant, You Should . . .

○ be able to follow instructions

○ be willing to do sometimes repetitive tasks

○ be organized and detailed oriented

○ have excellent people skills in order to work well with the public and coworkers

○ be a good problem solver

○ be comfortable working with technology

○ have a love of information

○ be prepared to master constantly changing technology

The Dewey Decimal Classification System

In the course of being employed as a student worker in his college library, and in visiting other libraries across the country, Melvil Dewey (1851–1931) began thinking about a unifying, decimal-based system of classifying books by subject rather than physical location in the library. He created the Dewey Decimal Classification (DDC) system in 1876. He was also a founding member of the American Library Association (1876) and founding editor of the *Library Journal* (1876–1880). Dewey also founded the first professional library school (1887).

The Dewey Decimal Classification system is the most widely used library classification system in the world. According to the OCLC Online Computer Library Center, the current owner of the system, the DDC system is used in the United States by 95 percent of all public and K–12 school libraries, 25 percent of college and university libraries, and 20 percent of special libraries. It has been translated into more than 30 languages.

Visit http://www.oclc.org/dewey to learn more about the Dewey Decimal Classification system.

2006. Salaries ranged from less than $14,070 to more than $34,810. On average, assistants working in special libraries that require technical knowledge have higher earning potential.

Outlook

According to the U.S. Department of Labor, the employment outlook for library assistants is good. Many of the jobs once handled by librarians, such as checking books in and out and reshelving and organizing materials, are

FOR MORE INFO

For career information, contact

American Library Association
50 East Huron Street
Chicago, IL 60611-2729
Tel: 800-545-2433
E-mail: library@ala.org
http://www.ala.org

To learn more about information science careers, contact

The American Society for Information Science & Technology
1320 Fenwick Lane, Suite 510
Silver Spring, MD 20910-3560
Tel: 301-495-0900
E-mail: asis@asis.org
http://www.asis.org

For information on working in a specialized library, contact

Special Libraries Association
331 South Patrick Street
Alexandria, VA 22314-3501
Tel: 703-647-4900
E-mail: sla@sla.org
http://www.sla.org

now being assigned to assistants and technicians. This should increase the demand for these positions, although it is important to note that full-time assistant positions are rare. Big metropolitan areas offer more opportunities for employment than smaller, rural areas. As is true in other fields, the more eager an individual is to learn and stay up to date with current technology, the greater his or her chances of finding employment.

Library Directors

What Library Directors Do

Library directors are the heads of library organizations. They are responsible for all library operations, such as planning and assessing the collection, overseeing staff development, and providing service to patrons. They manage and may train employees working in reference, collection development, technical services, cataloging, circulation, and other areas of the library. Library directors are also called *head librarians* or *library administrators*.

In addition to managing staff, library directors must also manage the various types of resources offered at the library. These include CD-ROMS, Internet information, and traditional media formats such as periodicals, magazines, and books.

Library directors work in four main types of libraries: public, school, academic, and special.

Public libraries range in size from the New York Public Library with millions and millions of volumes and 85 branch libraries to town libraries with 10,000 to 15,000 volumes. *Public library directors* direct and manage the staff and operations of these libraries. Their job is unique in that they must make sure information is made easily accessible to anyone

Facts About Public Libraries

In 2002, RC Research and Consulting surveyed 1,000 people over the age of 18 regarding their use of public libraries. Here are some of the results:

- Libraries were most often used for educational purposes (46 percent) and entertainment (46 percent).
- 62 percent had a library card.
- 91 percent believed that libraries would exist in the future—despite the ready availability of information on the Internet.

EXPLORING

○ You can get a taste of what this job entails by volunteering or obtaining a part-time job at your local library or school library. You will gain valuable hands-on experience, as well as an opportunity to interact with library directors and other library professionals.

○ Professional associations can also provide a wealth of information about this career. Visit the American Library Association's Web site (http://www.ala.org) for articles on different library careers and profiles of librarians already established in their fields.

○ You may also want to participate in online discussion groups to get an insider's view of this industry.

○ People interested in libraries and the work of librarians can join the American Library Association via a personal membership.

who holds a library card. This ranges from the fourth-grade student who is working on a book report, to a parent researching college financing, to a senior looking to make the most of retirement.

School library directors oversee the operation of a library hosted within a school. They work with their staff to help promote and encourage literacy and teach research skills so students can find information for school projects.

Although the job of *academic library director* may sound similar to that of school library director, the career is actually quite different. Academic libraries are found in colleges and universities, rather than local elementaries or high schools. These libraries range from a small college library with 10,000 volumes to a large university library with holdings of millions of volumes. Users range from college freshmen to university professors conducting research. Directors of these libraries oversee staff who document and store this important research and help students, professors, researchers, and other academics find and use this information.

Special libraries provide specialized information services to trade organizations, research laboratories, businesses, government agencies, art museums, hospitals, newspapers, publishers, and others. *Special library directors* manage the resources and employees in these libraries.

Education and Training

Take English, business, mathematics, computer science, and foreign languages in high school to prepare for this career.

Undergraduate training will vary depending on the type of library career you choose to pursue. Many library directors, especially those employed in a reference library, have a bachelor's degree in education. If you plan to become a director of a special library, then it would be wise to earn an undergraduate degree in a related field. Directors of corporate libraries, for example, often have degrees in business. Those who manage a music library may have a degree in music.

The director of special collections and archives at Wright State University displays some Wright brothers artifacts in the university's library. (Al Behrman, AP Photo)

All librarians, including library directors, must have a master's degree in library science (MLS/MLIS). Employers prefer to

To Be a Successful Library Director, You Should . . .

○ have a love of information

○ be organized

○ have good people skills

○ have good leadership skills

○ be a good communicator

○ have excellent financial management skills

○ be willing to continually learn about the field and new technologies

The Largest Library in the World

The Library of Congress, located in Washington, D.C., is the largest library in the world. It was created by an act of Congress in 1800. Here are some amazing facts about the Library of Congress in 2006:

○ More than 1.4 million people visited the library.

○ The library provided reference services to 633,396 individuals (in person, by telephone, and through written and electronic correspondence).

○ There were a total of 134,517,714 items in its collections.

○ Its Congressional Research Service completed 933,430 research assignments for members of Congress.

○ The library's Web sites recorded nearly 89 million visits, 458 million page views, and 4.6 billion "hits" on its public computer systems.

○ The library employed 3,783 permanent workers.

Visit http://www.loc.gov to learn more.

Source: The Library of Congress

hire graduates of programs accredited by the American Library Association. Larger libraries or university libraries require library directors to have a Ph.D. in library science or a related field.

Earnings

The American Library Association's Survey of Librarian Salaries reports the following mean annual salaries for managers in 2005: library directors, $78,054; deputy/associate/assistant directors, $60,729; department heads/coordinators/senior managers, $55,833; and managers/supervisors of support staff, $44,324.

Outlook

Employment opportunities for qualified library directors should be good. Although library directors will be in demand in a variety of library settings, the U.S. Department of Labor predicts that opportunities for library professionals will be best in nontraditional settings such as private corporations, non-profit organizations, and consulting firms. As for all careers, library directors with the most education and experience will have the best employment opportunities.

FOR MORE INFO

For career information and a list of accredited schools, contact
American Library Association
50 East Huron Street
Chicago, IL 60611-2729
Tel: 800-545-2433
E-mail: library@ala.org
http://www.ala.org

To learn more about information science careers, contact
The American Society for Information Science & Technology
1320 Fenwick Lane, Suite 510
Silver Spring, MD 20910-3560
Tel: 301-495-0900
E-mail: asis@asis.org
http://www.asis.org

For information on careers in library management, contact
Library Administration and Management Association
American Library Association

50 East Huron Street
Chicago, IL 60611-2729
Tel: 800-545-2433, ext. 5032
E-mail: lama@ala.org
http://www.ala.org/lama

For information on working in a specialized library, contact
Special Libraries Association
331 South Patrick Street
Alexandria, VA 22314-3501
Tel: 703-647-4900
E-mail: sla@sla.org
http://www.sla.org

To receive information on librarianship in Canada, contact
Canadian Library Association
328 Frank Street
Ottawa, ON K2P 0X8 Canada
Tel: 613-232-9625
E-mail: info@cla.ca
http://www.cla.ca

Library Media Specialists

What Library Media Specialists Do

Most school libraries use more resources than printed books and magazines to help students learn. Because so much information is now available on CD-ROMs, electronic encyclopedias, videos, DVDs, and the Internet, schools must use computers, compact disc players, DVD players, videotape machines, filmstrip projectors, and other equipment to access that information. *Library media specialists* help students and teachers use print and nonprint resources and equipment to find the information they need.

Library media specialists might teach people how to find information on the Internet or how to use a CD-ROM. They also share this information with teachers. Specialists might suggest special media projects to teachers and students and order cameras, slides, and other supplies for them.

In elementary schools, library media specialists provide activities geared to the educational needs of young students. For instance, they plan story hours and puppet shows designed to encourage reading. At all grade levels, specialists teach classes in how to run equipment

Library Facts and Figures

It is estimated that there are 117,378 libraries of all kinds in the United States today. These include:

- 93,861 school libraries
- 9,207 public libraries
- 9,181 special libraries (corporate, medical, law, religious, etc.)
- 3,653 academic libraries
- 1,174 government libraries
- 302 armed forces libraries

Source: American Library Association

such as slide and overhead projectors, and they might demonstrate an activity such as setting up a home page on the Internet.

Library media specialists are responsible for choosing new sources of information as well as the equipment needed to access that information. To select the materials best suited for their school, they read product descriptions, talk to salespeople, and inspect products. They must be familiar with new technologies. Once the materials arrive, they are responsible for organizing the resources in the library media center so that students and teachers can easily access the information.

In addition to researching and ordering materials, library media specialists also care for them. They check audiovisual aids in and out of the media center, inspect items for damage, and make any necessary repairs. If an item becomes severely damaged, the media specialist hires qualified repair people.

Education and Training

You should prepare for the field of library media by taking a strong college-preparatory course load in high school, including classes in English, science, foreign languages, history, geography, and mathematics. Additional study in communications, journalism, graphic

EXPLORING

○ Take part in a class in which a library media specialist teaches you how to use a CD-ROM to locate information in an encyclopedia. You may also work alone in the library media center, using the various print or audiovisual sources to complete a school project.

○ Volunteer to work in your school media programs.

○ Check to see if your school has a library club that you can join. If one doesn't exist, you could start your own.

○ Try to find summer or part-time employment with stores that sell audiovisual aids or companies that produce audiovisual equipment or software.

○ Talk to a library media specialist about his or her career. Ask the following questions: What are your main and secondary job duties? What do you like least and most about your job? How did you train for this field? What advice would you give a young person who is interested in the field?

To Be a Successful Library Media Specialist, You Should . . .

○ be familiar with many different print and nonprint resources

○ know how to operate all types of media equipment, especially computers

○ be creative in order to develop inventive ways to use media equipment to teach students

○ have good organizational and planning skills

○ enjoy working with children and young adults

○ be able to communicate well with many types of people

○ be able to handle responsibility and work well under pressure

○ be committed to learning throughout your career

arts, and computer science will give you good background knowledge of the materials you will use every day as a library media specialist.

After high school, you should earn an undergraduate degree in the liberal arts, educational media, or instructional technology. Although many library media specialists presently have only bachelor's degrees, the American Library Association recommends that entry-level library media specialist positions require a master's degree in library and information science.

Additionally, most states require library media specialists to be certified in education and in library media in order to work in public schools. Specialists must take the college courses and examinations necessary to receive teacher certification.

Earnings

Library media specialists had median annual earnings of $40,530 in 2006, according to the U.S. Department of Labor. Salaries ranged from less than $22,170 to more than $65,610 annually.

Outlook

More openings are expected in library media centers in schools, as well as in media centers in both public libraries and other organizations. As the use of computers continues to spread in classrooms and in library media centers, library media specialists who have developed excellent computer skills might move into positions such as computer coordinator for the entire school or school district.

Library media specialists who have worked in schools will also find opportunities to take their educational background into jobs with educational product companies as software producers or as researchers who help their firms determine the materials that schools need.

In addition, there will be increasing opportunities for library media specialists who wish to take their skills from the school and library setting into the outside world of business, industry, medical establishments, and government organizations. These alternative settings will allow experienced specialists to use media materials to train workers and to spread their messages to the public.

FOR MORE INFO

For career information and a list of accredited schools, contact
American Library Association
50 East Huron Street
Chicago, IL 60611-2729
Tel: 800-545-2433
E-mail: library@ala.org
http://www.ala.org

To obtain brochures pertaining to instructional materials and technology, contact
Association for Educational Communications and Technology
1800 North Stonelake Drive, Suite 2
Bloomington, IN 47404-1517
Tel: 877-677-2328
http://www.aect.org

Library Technicians

What Library Technicians Do

Library technicians help librarians or may work on their own to help people use the information stored in a library. They are employed by many different kinds of libraries, including school library media centers, university libraries, public libraries, and special libraries. The work performed by library technicians usually depends on the size and type of library. For instance, a technician working in a large public library might handle only one task, such as processing order forms for new books. A technician working in a small rural or special library might be the senior staff member, in charge of running the library and supervising other employees within the library.

Most work in libraries falls into one of two categories: working with library users or working behind the scenes maintaining the library. Library technicians work in both areas. When working with library users, they answer questions about the library and its services, and help people find what they need. Technicians may help people use audiovisual equipment, microfilm or microfiche machines, or computers. They may also work at the circulation desk, checking books in and out for patrons.

Millions and Millions of Books

The 10 largest libraries in the United States by volumes held are:

1. The Library of Congress	30,011,748
2. Harvard University	15,555,533
3. Boston Public Library	15,458,022
4. Yale University	12,025,695
5. University of Illinois–Urbana Champaign	10,370,777
6. County of Los Angeles Public Library	10,117,319
7. University of California–Berkeley	9,985,905
8. Columbia University	9,277,042
9. Public Library of Cincinnati and Hamilton County	9,148,846
10. University of Texas–Austin	8,937,002

Source: American Library Association

When working behind the scenes, library technicians help order books, register books for cataloging, organize and maintain the periodical collections, and use computer databases to gather information from other libraries. They might design posters, book displays, and bulletin boards to tell library users about special events and library services. They may also maintain and repair audiovisual equipment and oversee stack workers who put books back in the correct places on the shelves.

Technicians who work in administrative services help with the management of the library. They might help prepare budgets, coordinate the efforts of different departments within the library, write policy and procedures, and work to develop the library's collection.

Education and Training

Smaller libraries, especially those in rural areas, may hire people with only a high school education to be library technicians. Useful high school courses for future library technicians include English language and literature, foreign languages, and math. You should also take computer courses if they are available at your school. These classes will help you learn about how to deal with the materials in the library.

Many libraries require library technicians to be graduates of two-year associate's degree programs. The typical program includes courses that explain the basic purpose and function

EXPLORING

○ You can get a good idea of the general atmosphere of a library by using the library yourself. This will give you an idea of the types of services that a library provides for its patrons.

○ Visit a large or specialized library to learn about the different kinds of libraries that exist.

○ Work as a library volunteer at a public library or in the school library media center.

○ Some grammar schools or high schools offer library clubs as extra-curricular activities. If your school doesn't have a library club, contact your school librarian and gather some friends to start your own group.

○ Talk with your school or community librarians and library technicians about their careers.

○ Part-time or summer work as a shelving clerk or typist may also be available in some libraries.

A library technician assists a caller. (Rachel Epstein, The Image Works)

of libraries; book and magazine ordering; materials processing; user services; and Internet use. Such a program also includes a year of liberal arts courses.

Earnings

Salaries for library technicians vary depending on such factors as the type of library, geographic location, and specific job responsibilities. According to the U.S. Department of Labor, the median annual salary for all library technicians in 2006 was $26,560. Salaries ranged from less than $15,820 to more than $42,850. Library technicians employed by the federal government earned mean annual salaries of $40,740 in 2006.

Outlook

Employment for library technicians will grow about as fast as the average, according to the U.S. Department of Labor.

To Be a Successful Library Technician, You Should . . .

- be able to follow instructions
- be good at detailed work
- enjoy problem solving
- like working with people as well as with books and other library materials
- be patient and flexible
- have excellent time management skills
- be able to work as a member of a team

Famous Libraries on the Web

Boston Public Library
http://www.bpl.org

The British Library
http://www.bl.uk

Carnegie Library of Pittsburgh
http://www.carnegielibrary.org

Chicago Public Library
http://www.chipublib.org

Harvard University Library
http://hul.harvard.edu

The Library of Congress
http://www.loc.gov/homepage/lchp.html

The New York Public Library
http://www.nypl.org

Yale University Library
http://www.library.yale.edu

Job openings will result from technicians leaving the field for other employment or retirement, as well as from libraries looking to stretch their budgets. Since a library technician earns less than a librarian, a library may find it less expensive to hire the technician. The continued growth of special libraries in medical, business, and law organizations will lead to growing opportunities for technicians who develop specialized skills. A technician who has excellent computer skills and is able to learn quickly will have great employment prospects, as will a technician who shows the drive to gain advanced degrees and accept more responsibility.

FOR MORE INFO

For career information and a list of accredited schools, contact

American Library Association
50 East Huron Street
Chicago, IL 60611-2729
Tel: 800-545-2433
E-mail: library@ala.org
http://www.ala.org

To obtain brochures pertaining to instructional materials and technology, contact

Association for Educational Communications and Technology
1800 North Stonelake Drive, Suite 2
Bloomington, IN 47404-1517
Tel: 877-677-2328
http://www.aect.org

For information on working in a specialized library, contact

Special Libraries Association
331 South Patrick Street
Alexandria, VA 22314-3501
Tel: 703-647-4900
E-mail: sla@sla.org
http://www.sla.org

Medical Librarians

What Medical Librarians Do

Medical librarians, also called *medical information specialists,* help doctors, patients, and other medical workers find health information and select materials best suited to their needs.

Much of a medical librarian's job is similar to the work of a traditional librarian. He or she organizes, shelves, and helps people retrieve materials. Medical librarians may also help people check out materials, collect fines for overdue items, look for or reshelve misshelved items, and work with electronic media on CD-ROMs, DVDs, or the Internet.

Some medical librarians do not deal with the public at all. Instead, they work on the more technical tasks of ordering, cataloging, and classifying materials. These librarians select and order media for the library, evaluating newly published materials as well as seeking out older ones. In addition to traditional books and magazines, modern medical libraries also contain electronic records, DVDs, films, filmstrips, slides, and photographs. The selection and purchase of these is also the responsibility of the *head medical librarian.*

Medical acquisitions librarians choose and buy books and other media for the library. They read product catalogs and reviews of new materials as part

Where Do They Work?

- ○ hospitals
- ○ medical schools
- ○ university medical centers
- ○ consumer health libraries
- ○ large public libraries
- ○ businesses such as pharmaceutical, publishing, insurance, and biotechnology companies
- ○ nonprofit organizations
- ○ government agencies (Centers for Disease Control, National Institutes of Health, Department of Health and Human Services)
- ○ anyplace that has a collection of health information

EXPLORING

○ As a student, you probably use the library all the time—and if you don't, you should! Make the most of your public and school libraries when working on papers and other projects.

○ Check out career resources about medical librarianship. The Medical Library Association offers brochures, a career video, and other resources at its Web site, http://www.mlanet.org/career.

○ Contact the Medical Library Association, the American Library Association, and other professional library organizations to inquire about student memberships.

○ Ask at local libraries or your school library to see if they need an assistant or part-time worker or volunteer. The experience you gain will be useful in the future.

of the acquisitions decision process. They do not work with the public, but deal with publishers, wholesalers, booksellers, and distributors. When the ordered materials arrive, *medical catalog librarians,* with the aid of *medical classifiers,* classify the items by medical field, assign classification numbers, and prepare computer records to help users locate the materials. Since libraries have computerized the acquisitions and cataloging functions, it is now possible for the user to retrieve materials faster.

Medical bibliographers usually work in research libraries, compiling lists of books, periodicals, articles, and audiovisual materials on selected topics in the health field. They also recommend the purchase of new materials.

Education and Training

If you are interested in becoming a medical librarian, be sure to take a full college-preparatory course load in high school. Focus on classes such as anatomy, biology, chemistry, and physics. Learning how to use a computer and conduct basic research in a library is essential.

You will need to earn a master's degree to become a librarian. The degree is generally known as a master's of library science (MLS), but in some institutions it may be referred to by a different title, such as a master's of library and information science (MLIS). You should plan to attend a graduate school that is accredited by the American Library Association.

Because they work with such specialized materials, medical librarians must have a very strong background in the area in which they wish to work. Most medical librarians have a degree in science in addition to their MLS. In some cases, a graduate or professional degree in the sciences is especially attractive to prospective employers. For work in research libraries, university libraries, or special collections, a doctorate may be required. A doctorate is commonly required for the top administrative posts at these types of libraries. It is also required for faculty positions in graduate schools of library science.

Earnings

Salaries depend on such factors as the amount of experience the medical librarian has, the responsibilities of the position, and the location, size, and type of library. The Medical Library Association reports that the average starting salary for medical librarians with less than two years of experience was $40,832

To Be a Successful Medical Librarian, You Should . . .

○ be knowledgeable about medical and health issues

○ have excellent communication skills

○ be a good problem solver

○ be patient

○ have good listening skills

○ enjoy teaching people

○ be an expert at computers and other technology

○ have perseverance in order to find difficult-to-locate information

○ be willing to continue to learn about the field throughout your career

FOR MORE INFO

For career information and a list of accredited schools, contact

American Library Association
50 East Huron Street
Chicago, IL 60611-2729
Tel: 800-545-2433
E-mail: library@ala.org
http://www.ala.org

To learn more about information science careers, contact

The American Society for Information Science & Technology
1320 Fenwick Lane, Suite 510
Silver Spring, MD 20910-3560
Tel: 301-495-0900
E-mail: asis@asis.org
http://www.asis.org

For information on careers in medical librarianship, contact

Medical Library Association
65 East Wacker Place, Suite 1900
Chicago, IL 60601-7246
Tel: 312-419-9094
E-mail: info@mlahq.org
http://www.mlanet.org

For information on working in a specialized library, contact

Special Libraries Association
331 South Patrick Street
Alexandria, VA 22314-3501
Tel: 703-647-4900
E-mail: sla@sla.org
http://www.sla.org

in 2005. The average salary for all medical librarians regardless of experience was $57,892 in 2005. Medical library supervisors can earn between $60,000 and $158,000 annually.

Outlook

More than two million health-related articles and 24,000 medical journals and related publications are published annually. Individuals trained to catalog and organize this information are in strong demand and will continue to be in demand in the next decade—especially due to predicted shortages of librarians in the coming years.

Music Librarians

What Music Librarians Do

Music librarians perform many of the same tasks as general librarians. These duties, with an emphasis on music, include arranging, cataloging, and maintaining library collections; helping patrons find materials and advising them on how to use resources effectively; creating catalogs, indexes, brochures, exhibits, Web sites, and bibliographies to educate users about the library's resources; supervising the purchase and maintenance of the equipment needed to use these materials; hiring, training, and supervising library staff; setting and implementing budgets; and keeping abreast of developments in the field. They also select and acquire music, videotapes, records, cassettes, DVDs, compact discs, books, manuscripts, and other nonbook materials for the library. This involves evaluating newly published materials as well as seeking out older materials.

Specialized duties for music librarians vary based on their employer and their skills. For example, a music librarian employed by a college, university, or conservatory may acquire the music needed by student musical groups. A librarian who is employed by a music publisher may help edit musical publications. Music librarians employed by radio and television stations catalog and oversee music-related materials that are used by the employees of these organizations.

Where Do They Work?

- music libraries
- large research libraries such as the Library of Congress
- colleges and universities
- conservatories
- public and private libraries
- archives
- radio and television stations
- musical societies and foundations
- professional bands and orchestras
- music publishing companies
- military

EXPLORING

○ Ask your school librarian to direct you to books and other resources about music and library careers.

○ Contact the Music Library Association or the American Library Association (see For More Info) to inquire about student memberships. Many library associations offer excellent mentoring opportunities as well.

○ Some schools may have library clubs you can join to learn about library work. If one doesn't exist, you could start your own.

○ Try to take as many music-related classes as possible in high school. These will begin to give you the basic framework you need to become a music librarian.

○ Ask your school librarian to help you learn more about music librarian careers. Perhaps he or she took a music librarianship course in college or has a colleague who specializes in the field.

○ Work as an assistant in the school library media center or find part-time work in a local public library.

They research and recommend music selections for programs, pull and refile musical selections for on-air shifts, and maintain relationships with record companies and distributors.

Some music librarians arrange special music-related courses, presentations, or performances at their libraries. They may also create lists of books, periodicals, articles, and audiovisual materials on music, or they may teach others how to do this.

Music librarians at large libraries may specialize in one particular task. *Music catalogers* are librarians who specialize in the cataloging and classification of music-related materials such as scores and sound recordings, software, audiovisual materials, and books. *Music bibliographers* create detailed lists of music-related materials for use by library patrons. They may organize these lists by subject, language, date, composer, musician, or other criteria.

In addition to their regular duties, some music librarians teach music or library science–related courses at colleges and universities. Others write reviews of books and music for print and online publications.

Education and Training

If you are interested in becoming a music librarian, be sure to take classes in music, English, speech, history, and foreign languages in high school. Be sure also to take classes that help you develop your computer and research skills.

Most students interested in becoming music librarians pursue undergraduate education in a music-related field, such as musicology, music education, music theory/composition, or vocal and instrumental performance. In addition to music-related courses, be sure to take at least one foreign language since music and music literature are published in many languages.

You will need to earn a master's degree to become a librarian. The degree is generally known as the master of library science (MLS), but in some institutions it may be referred to by a different title, such as the master of library and information science (MLIS). You should plan to attend a graduate school of library and information science that is accredited by the American Library Association.

A second master's degree in music is usually required for the best music librarianship positions. Some schools offer a dual

Music Firsts

○ The oldest known musical notation appears on a Mesopotamian cuneiform tablet from about 1800 BC.

○ In the United States, the first music library was established by the Brooklyn (New York) Public Library in 1882.

○ The Library of Congress Division of Music was organized in the 1890s, with a phonorecord collection established at the institution in 1903.

○ In 1931, the Music Library Association was formed to represent the professional interests of music librarians.

To Be a Successful Music Librarian, You Should . . .

○ have a deep love of music
○ have an excellent memory and a keen eye for detail
○ be willing to assist patrons with difficult requests
○ get along well with others
○ have a good imagination
○ be highly motivated
○ be a good problem solver

FOR MORE INFO

For career information and a list of accredited schools, contact
American Library Association
50 East Huron Street
Chicago, IL 60611-2729
Tel: 800-545-2433
E-mail: library@ala.org
http://www.ala.org

For information on careers and educational options in music librarianship, contact
Music Library Association
8551 Research Way, Suite 180
Middleton, WI 53562-3567
Tel: 608-836-5825
http://www.musiclibraryassoc.org

For information on working in a specialized library, contact
Special Libraries Association
331 South Patrick Street
Alexandria, VA 22314-3501
Tel: 703-647-4900
E-mail: sla@sla.org
http://www.sla.org

degree in librarianship and music. Common combinations include an MLS with either a master of arts in musicology, a master of music in music history, or a master of music in music theory.

A doctorate may be required for work in research libraries, university libraries, or special collections. A doctorate is commonly required for the top administrative posts in these types of libraries. It is also required for faculty positions in graduate schools of library science.

Earnings

Salaries for music librarians depend on such factors as the applicant's experience; the location, size, and type of library; and the responsibilities of the position. No current salary information is available for music librarians. According to the U.S. Department of Labor, median annual earnings of all librarians in 2006 were $49,060. Salaries ranged from less than $30,930 to more than $74,670. Librarians working in colleges and universities averaged about $53,930 in 2006.

Outlook

Employment for music librarians is expected to grow more slowly than the average. The field of musical librarianship is small, and there is little turnover in the best positions. Music librarians with advanced education and knowledge of more than one foreign language will have the best employment prospects.

Research Assistants

What Research Assistants Do

Research assistants help find facts, information, and statistics. They work for scientists, editors and writers, publishers, film-makers, attorneys, and advertising executives, among others. Today, almost every field imaginable hires research assistants to help get jobs done more thoroughly and quickly.

After they receive an assignment, research assistants decide how to find information. They may spend hours, days, or even weeks of research in archives, libraries, laboratories, museums; on the Internet; or in conversation with experts. Research assistants write up notes or a report of the information.

Research assistants who work for writers or editors help find statistics or other information for a specific article or book. Some research assistants called *fact-checkers* make sure that facts, such as dates, ages, and numbers, are correct before they are published. Research assistants who work in radio, film, and television might help to find and verify historical information or locate experts to be interviewed. Research assistants who work in the sciences, engineering, or medicine help scientists find background information for their experiments.

University professors hire research assistants, often graduate students, to help them in their research. For example, a history professor working on a paper about the Italian military might send a research assistant to the library to uncover everything possible about the Italian military presence in Greece during World War II (1939–1945).

Advertising agencies and marketing departments hire research assistants to help them decide how and when a product should be sold.

Law firms hire research assistants to find out facts about past cases and laws.

Politicians hire research assistants to help find out how a campaign is succeeding or failing, to find statistics on outcomes of past elections, and to determine the issues that are especially important to the constituents.

Education and Training

History, English, mathematics, and foreign language classes are good preparation for this career. Pay special attention to your writing and research skills. Since electronic research is becoming more important, you should take classes in computers and Internet research techniques. If you are interested in science and engineering research, you should take all the laboratory courses you can.

Education requirements vary, depending on the field in which you work as a research assistant. Most employers require an undergraduate degree. Some fields, especially the sciences, engineering, and law, may require you to have an advanced degree or other special training.

Earnings

Salaries for research assistants vary, depending on the field of research and the size and resources of the employer. Those who

EXPLORING

○ Experiment with different types of research using newspapers, magazines, library catalogs, computers, the Internet, and official records and documents.
○ Ask a librarian or bookstore clerk to help you find books on how to do research. A resource librarian would be glad to talk to you about the many research tools you can use.
○ Work as a reporter for your school newspaper, or volunteer to write feature articles for your yearbook. You can research the history of your school, the history of its sports programs, or famous alumni.

To Be a Successful Research Assistant, You Should . . .

○ have a curious nature
○ be resourceful
○ be good at finding and organizing information
○ enjoy working with other people
○ be able to handle multiple tasks
○ be self-motivated
○ be able to follow instructions

earn the highest salaries often work in the sciences for large companies or laboratories such as in the pharmaceutical industry.

Research assistants who work part time for a professor while earning a graduate degree generally earn about $12,500 a year. Full-time research assistants earn from about $25,000 to $52,000 a year.

Have You Got What It Takes?

See if you've got what it takes to be a top-notch researcher. Be creative and try to find the following information:

○ Where did George Washington, the first president of the United States, attend college?
○ How many lumberjacks does the government currently employ?
○ How many species of animals become extinct every day? Each year?
○ How many current National Football League players earned a college degree before turning professional?
○ Who holds the world record for plate spinning?
○ How many number one songs has Neil Diamond recorded? Of those, how many did he write?

Outlook

The job outlook varies depending on the field. A researcher with good background in many fields will be in higher demand, as will a researcher with specialized knowledge and research techniques specific to a field. The best opportunities will be for highly skilled research assistants who are trained in the sciences.

FOR MORE INFO

To learn more about information science careers, contact
The American Society for Information Science & Technology
1320 Fenwick Lane, Suite 510
Silver Spring, MD 20910-3560
Tel: 301-495-0900
E-mail: asis@asis.org
http://www.asis.org

To learn more about opportunities in the field, contact
Association of Independent Information Professionals
8550 United Plaza Boulevard, Suite 1001

Baton Rouge, LA 70809-0200
Tel: 225-408-4400
Email: info@aiip.org
http://www.aiip.org/index.html

Visit the following Web site for useful resources for researchers
The Library of Congress Researchers: Reference Tools and Services
http://lcweb.loc.gov/rr

For information on research assistant positions with the U.S. Census Bureau, visit
U.S. Census Bureau
http://www.census.gov

Glossary

accredited approved as meeting established standards for providing good training and education. This approval is usually given by an independent organization of professionals.

apprentice a person who is learning a trade by working under the supervision of a skilled worker. Apprentices often receive classroom instruction in addition to their supervised practical experience.

associate's degree an academic rank or title granted by a community or junior college or similar institution to graduates of a two-year program of education beyond high school.

bachelor's degree an academic rank or title given to a person who has completed a four-year program of study at a college or university. Also called an undergraduate degree or baccalaureate.

career an occupation for which a worker receives training and has an opportunity for advancement.

certified approved as meeting established requirements for skill, knowledge, and experience in a particular field. People are certified by the organization of professionals in their field.

college a higher education institution that is above the high school level.

community college a public or private two-year college attended by students who do not usually live at the college. Graduates of a community college receive an associate's degree and may transfer to a four-year college or university to complete a bachelor's degree.

diploma a certificate or document given by a school to show that a person has completed a course or has graduated from the school.

distance education a type of educational program that allows students to take classes and complete their education by mail or the Internet.

doctorate the highest academic rank or title granted by a graduate school to a person who has completed a program after having received a master's degree.

fringe benefit a payment or benefit to an employee in addition to regular wages or salary. Examples of fringe benefits include a pension, a paid vacation, and health or life insurance.

graduate school a school that people may attend after receiving their bachelor's degree. People who complete an educational program at a graduate school earn a master's degree or a doctorate.

intern an advanced student (usually one with at least some college training) in a professional field who is employed in a job that is intended to provide supervised practical experience for the student.

internship 1. the position or job of an intern. 2. the period of time when a person is an intern.

junior college a two-year college that offers courses like those in the first half of a four-year college program. Graduates of a junior college usually receive an associate's degree and may transfer to a four-year college or university to complete a bachelor's degree.

liberal arts the subjects covered by college courses that develop broad general knowledge rather than specific occupational skills. The liberal arts are often considered to include philosophy, literature and the arts, history, language, and some courses in the social sciences and natural sciences.

major (in college) the academic field in which a student specializes and receives a degree.

master's degree an academic rank or title granted by a graduate school to a person who has completed a program after having received a bachelor's degree.

pension an amount of money paid regularly by an employer to a former employee after he or she retires from working.

scholarship a gift of money to a student to help the student pay for further education.

social studies courses of study (such as civics, geography, and history) that deal with how human societies work.

starting salary annual pay for a newly hired employee. The starting salary is usually a smaller amount than is paid to a more experienced worker.

technical college a private or public college offering two- or four-year programs in technical subjects. Technical colleges offer courses in both general and technical subjects and award associate's degrees and bachelor's degrees.

undergraduate a student at a college or university who has not yet received a degree.

undergraduate degree See bachelor's degree.

union an organization whose members are workers in a particular industry or company. The union works to gain better wages, benefits, and working conditions for its members. Also called a labor union or trade union.

vocational school a public or private school that offers training in one or more skills or trades.

wage money that is paid in return for work done, especially money paid on the basis of the number of hours or days worked.

Index of Job Titles

Browse and Learn More

Books

Eberts, Marjorie, and Margaret Gisler. *Careers for Bookworms & Other Literary Types.* 3d ed. New York: McGraw-Hill, 2002.

Fourie, Denise K., and David R. Dowell. *Libraries in the Information Age: An Introduction and Career Exploration.* Westport, Conn.: Libraries Unlimited, 2002.

Gordon, Rachel Singer. *The Nextgen Librarian's Survival Guide.* Medford, N.J.: Information Today, 2006.

Kane, Laura Townsend. *Straight from the Stacks: A Firsthand Guide to Careers in Library and Information Science.* Chicago: American Library Association, 2003.

Keane, Nancy J. *The Big Book of Teen Reading Lists: 100 Great, Ready-to-Use Book Lists for Educators, Librarians, Parents, and Teens.* Westport, Conn.: Libraries Unlimited, 2006.

Lerner, Fred. *Libraries Through the Ages.* New York: Continuum, 1999.

Myers, Margaret, and Kathleen de la Pena McCook. *Opportunities in Library and Information Science Careers.* New York: McGraw-Hill, 2001.

Pearl, Nancy. *Book Crush: For Kids and Teens: Recommended Reading for Every Mood, Moment, and Interest.* Seattle: Sasquatch Books, 2007.

Peterson's Summer Opportunities for Kids & Teenagers. 24th ed. Lawrenceville, N.J.: Peterson's, 2006.

Sawa, Maureen. *The Library Book: The Story of Libraries from Camels to Computers.* Plattsburgh, N.Y.: Tundra Books, 2006.

Schlein, Alan M. *Find It Online: The Complete Guide to Online Research.* 4th ed. Tempe, Ariz.: Facts on Demand Press, 2004.

Shontz, Priscilla K. *Jump Start Your Career in Library and Information Science.* Lanham, Md.: The Scarecrow Press, 2002.

Shontz, Priscilla K., and Richard A. Murray, eds. *A Day in the Life: Career Options in Library and Information Science.* Westport, Conn.: Libraries Unlimited, 2007.

Wilkinson, Frances C., and Linda K. Lewis. *The Complete Guide to Acquisitions Management.* Westport, Conn.: Libraries Unlimited, 2003.

Web Sites

American Library Association

http://www.ala.org

American Library Association: Great Web Sites for Kids

http://www.ala.org/greatsites

Dewey Decimal Classification

http://www.oclc.org/dewey

Finding Data on the Internet

http://www.robertniles.com/data

KYVL for Kids

http://www.kyvl.org/html/kids/portal.html

LibraryCareers.org

http://www.ala.org/ala/hrdr/librarycareerssite/whatyouneed.htm

The Library of Congress: America's Story from America's Library

http://www.americaslibrary.gov/cgi-bin/page.cgi

The Library of Congress: Kids and Families

http://www.loc.gov/families

The Library History Buff

http://www.libraryhistorybuff.org

Music Librarianship: Is It For You?

http://www.musiclibraryassoc.org/employmentanded/music librarianship.shtml

The New York Public Library "On-Lion" for Kids

http://kids.nypl.org